JESUS AND THE
FUNDAMENTALISM OF HIS DAY

Jesus and the
Fundamentalism of His Day

• •

William Loader

William B. Eerdmans Publishing Company
Grand Rapids, Michigan / Cambridge, U.K.

Wm. B. Eerdmans Publishing Co.
255 Jefferson Ave. S.E., Grand Rapids, Michigan 49503 /
P.O. Box 163, Cambridge CB3 9PU U.K.

Printed in the United States of America

05 04 03 02 01   5 4 3 2 1

Library of Congress Cataloging-in-Publication Data

Loader, William R. G., 1944-
Jesus and the fundamentalism of his day / William Loader.
p.   cm.
Includes bibliographical references and index.
ISBN 0-8028-4796-X (pbk.: alk. paper)
1. Jesus Christ — Conflicts. 2. Bible. N.T. Gospels — Criticism,
interpretation, etc. 3. Deconstruction.   I. Title.
BT303.L63   2001
226'.06 — dc21

00-049468

www.eerdmans.com

Contents

Introduction

It caught me by surprise — but there they were: gum trees on the shores of Capernaum! Disembarking from the ferry I could reach out, pluck a eucalyptus leaf, and suddenly smell that "at home" feeling as I rubbed it in my hands. A little bit of Australia in Jesus' hometown. But then it might seem equally strange that in the land of the eucalyptus we find the story of the carpenter of Galilee and the signs of the movement his life created. It is already fantastic that his first-century movement is alive and well in the twenty-first century. The tradition of Jesus has transplanted itself in ever new generations and has taken up roots in strange soil.

Walking down the road from the jetty I am reminded that there is much more to it. There at the end of the road are remnants of a synagogue erected a few centuries after Jesus. Underneath are signs of an earlier building constructed from local stone. It was here that Jesus proclaimed the gospel. It was possibly here or in a similar meeting place in his hometown Nazareth that he heard the great stories of the Old Testament. This place is full of history. It is full of culture, especially Jewish culture. Even two thousand years later you can feel something of what Jesus must have felt as he looked out at those same hills and over that same lake. Some things have not changed. Silt and the occasional earthquake have changed the shoreline. Neighboring Bethsaida to the east is no longer on the shore. The Jordan has been building its alluvial plain; but, even so the fish are still there along with the fishing industry.

1

Change and Continuity

Change and continuity. Change of time and change of place. Change of culture. Across time and space Christians acclaim continuity and all that Jesus stood for. Jesus is alive even as the twentieth century merges into a new millennium. The exiles of Israel asked, "How can we worship God in a strange land?" We might ask: How can we discern and do God's will in a place and time so distant from the age when Jesus walked these streets? How much of the ancient tradition preserved in Scripture is still just as relevant for today and how much belongs to the language and customs of yesteryear?

This book is about how we read the Bible, how we handle the religious tradition we have inherited, and how we sort out what matters most from what matters little or not at all. It has been common for people who argue for sensitivity to such distinctions to point to Paul's instruction to the Corinthians that women should worship with their hair covered. Few within the church insist on such practices today, although the issue has reentered Australia in a new form. Many women in our Islamic communities apply strict rules about covering to everyday life. Within the churches we have learned to treat such demands lightly and to respect them as observances belonging to a particular cultural experience rather than as universal rules.

The film *Chariots of Fire* was a splendid illustration of devout sabbath observance applied to Sunday. Yet within a few decades strict Sunday observance has been modified to the point that we find religious institutions — the same ones that once sanctioned great strictness about sport on Sundays — blessing, and sometimes running, Sunday leisure programs. Some will see this as a sign of depravity. If people think about it at all — and few do — they do not see this as a depravity, but as a result of reassessing our attitudes towards Scripture and tradition. Divorce is a more serious case in point. A good many Christians and Christian churches see it as frequently presenting the most creative and caring option for all concerned. Again, they would not see this as a sign of lax morality; rather the issue has become one of what is most practical and compassionate.

How Much Change?

Just how far should such changes go? Are we in danger of throwing away what Scripture stands for? Does its authority no longer stand? How can you say you acknowledge the Bible's authority and in the next step sanction divorce? These are legitimate questions, and they are based on fears that must be taken seriously. When Paul warned Roman Christians not to be conformed to the world, he was making it clear that the world, the predominant culture of any age, exerts enormous pressure to make everyone conform. Just look how fashions govern the lives of so many. A Christianity that conforms itself to the going fashions is likely to disappear into the sand. It will lose its distinctiveness and end up becoming the religious justification for the dominant culture. In its history it has been hard for Christianity, especially in the West, not to succumb to this temptation. When it does so, it runs the risk of disappearing as cultural values change.

The issue of what abides and what can be left aside as belonging to past culture and custom lies behind many of the disputes that face the churches today. It has comes to the fore in discussions about women in the church and in ministry, and in the churches' grappling with sexuality and homosexuality in particular. It is also there at a deeper level in ways people think about God, about Jesus, and about the church. How can we hang on to what is vital and let go what is not vital? And how can we tell the difference?

Jesus and Change

This book is about the way Jesus dealt with such issues and the way those who told his story reflected on it. It is written in the hope that understanding what went on then will shed light on ways of handling the issues today. People too often assume that to interpret and reinterpret Scripture in the light of changed realities or changed perceptions of reality is a modern phenomenon. It is not. It was a central issue in Jesus' disputes with his contemporaries and continued to be central in the church of New Testament times. Those who opposed such an approach to Scripture and insisted on keeping to the letter of its demands were to be found mostly not on the side of Jesus but among his opponents. This was, indeed, one of the major reasons why many opposed him and later opposed people like Paul from within Christianity. Thus passions aroused in our day were also aroused on the streets of first-century Capernaum and in those early Christian communities that first heard the gospels. The emergence of Christianity within Judaism had a lot to do with the way people treated the Scriptures. The very existence of Christianity depended in part on a particular solution to these problems.

The people who followed Jesus were real people. They were committed, devout, and energetic in their proclamation of the story of Jesus. But they soon scattered far and wide outside of Galilee. As soon as they did, the issue arose: Was their Jewishness an essential part of their being Christians or did it need to be jettisoned? Few chose either of these extremes. Most grappled with compromise solutions. The passion of the conflicts that arose was because they did not see this as a matter of holding or discarding Jewish customs; they saw it as observing or discarding commands of Scripture. When Paul championed the view that Gentiles need not be circumcised he laid himself open to the charge that he was rejecting the explicit command of Scripture; and in fact the accusers were correct. Fortunately there were others who supported Paul's stance in this, but even among them there were fierce disputes. Some felt that Paul had gone far too far in saying Christians are no longer under the Law. After the clash between Peter and Paul in Antioch over observing biblical laws concerning food, most sided with Peter. These were struggles going on within Christianity.

About the Bible

It is little surprise that two millennia later we find similar passions aroused when people differ on how to treat the Bible. It was not that Paul or Peter or James or the strict fundamentalist Jewish Christians who allowed no compromise had a low view of Scripture. They all hailed its authority and saw at as holy. They even argued on the basis of its authority when supporting the various stands they adopted. But their approaches varied.

The more extreme group argued that every statement was inspired, every command infallible. It was a very logical and consistent stance. The Bible is the Word of God and that is that; no changes! It would have been hard to answer. These people would see Jesus as the climax of God's action in the world, but not as one who rendered actions and instructions of the past obsolete or inapplicable. God has acted consistently throughout. Those who claimed otherwise laid themselves open to the charge that they were watering down the commands of Scripture and that they were being inconsistent — and declaring God to be inconsistent. Waiving the clear demand that non-Jews be circumcised was especially suspect. How could you answer the accusation that this was a very crude case of cheap marketing by dropping standards?

Nonetheless most of the early Christian movement espoused this more lenient approach and rejected the suggestion that it was a cheap ploy. They were forced to develop a different way of interpreting Scripture. They rejected the view that all Scripture commands are equal because they are all God's commands. In various ways they argued that some commandments were less important than others and that some could even be discarded. The more they made Jesus the center of their thinking about God, the easier it became to claim that his coming had necessitated a change. Still, there were others who rejected this. They saw nothing in Jesus that required any such changes.

We are fortunate to possess a number of Paul's original letters, which reflect these conflicts. Most of them stem from the time when Christianity was only about two decades old. They are worth reading for their own sake, and they reveal the depth of the conflict at that early stage. Some of this is still evident in the account of early Christianity written about thirty years later in the Acts of the Apostles.

The Gospels

In this book I shall be looking particularly at the gospels. They are the primary sources about Jesus and so help us understand the conflicts he faced. They also indicate how four different writers understood the issues in their own time. This has the advantage of enabling us to set these pictures of Jesus side by side. There is not one single approach to the use of Scripture in the New Testament, and there is not one single way of understanding how Jesus approached the matter and, by implication, how we should do so. There are at least four. By looking at these different approaches in some detail we shall be able also to compare and contrast them. In the process it is my hope that we may come to a better understanding of what the issues are in interpreting Scripture today. There are four different approaches, but also some significant common elements.

Another advantage of approaching the issue this way is that, hopefully, we will avoid the generalizations that often dog discussion of the role of Scripture, frequently with dogmatic claim and counterclaim, and too often (on both sides) without adequately listening to what the biblical writings themselves say. Instead, I am inviting the reader right into the text. Let us hear what each gospel writing is saying. Let us try to get in touch with what the issues were then.

Of the four gospels, Mark is commonly believed to be the earliest, written around the year 70. Matthew and Luke wrote about fifteen years later. They revised and expanded Mark. They also appear to have used another written source that has not survived, standardly identified by the letter Q. John's gospel stands on its own and has been produced independently of the others, although the author may have known them at a distance. In 1947 a further gospel came to light, the Gospel of Thomas, a collection of sayings of Jesus. In its final form it comes from the second century but appears to be based on a much earlier collection.

Each of these gospels deals in its own way with the issue of continuity and change. This probably reflects to a large degree what was going on in the communities in which their authors wrote. Each contains sayings and anecdotes about Jesus that are much older than the gospels themselves. Many of these earlier traditions also reflect the struggles in the early church communities over the way to treat the Bible. A good many of them give us insight into the approach of Jesus on the matter. It was, after all, a major source of controversy in his ministry. When the churches find themselves in passionate controversy about how to interpret the Bible they are in good company. It went on in the apostolic age. It was a major issue in the ministry of Jesus.

Fundamentalism?

The title of this book uses the word "Fundamentalism." Strictly speaking, the term arose in relation to a twentieth-century phenomenon. But, as is the case with words, the term is now used much more widely. It is one of the flags people wave in the debate over Scripture — for some, a term of abuse, for others, a key tenet of faith. I am using it in the popular sense to refer to an approach to interpreting Scripture that accepts it without question as absolute authority, leaving no room for taking into account changed circumstances or possible error. Such an approach is often characterized by a concentration on the letter of Scripture as law and as binding for all time, and stands in contrast to another approach that interprets the authority of Scripture for what it enshrines and the attitudes it purveys.

Both approaches may apply the term "Word of God" to the Bible, but in the former case the meaning is closer to "the words of God." It is often linked to speculation about how the limited nature of the writers as human beings had been overridden to prevent error and ensure absolute authority. Both approaches may speak of inspiration, but, again, in the former case the inspiration often tends towards being a theory about how human words or statements could be deemed divine and inerrant. No doubt Jesus and Paul considered that God's word was to be heard in the Scriptures and that they were the products of God's Spirit in the lives of people, but the authority is located at a deeper level. It is not seen as overriding natural human limitations, whether in relation to factual inaccuracies or in relation to reflecting the limited knowledge and perspectives of one particular cultural or religious background.

Dangers

There are two notes of caution. First, it is a common mistake to assume that fundamentalism is a monolithic system of thought. Many people are fundamentalist in their attitude towards Scripture because that is part of the culture in which they have grown up. They are not ideologically fundamentalist and move easily from an uncritical appreciation of Scripture to a more discerning approach. Often, their approach to the Bible is just an element of their spirituality, which may be very open, flexible, and compassionate. To cast labels on people who happen to have grown up in such an environment is to my mind both inappropriate and frequently destructive.

Others, however, who deliberately espouse what I have described as a fundamentalist approach to Scripture frequently use the term of themselves and it is an appropriate description for the attitude they espouse. Even then I would want to caution that it is easy to slip from discussing fundamentalism as an approach, one of my concerns in this book, to discussing people as fundamentalists. People are always more than whatever "-ist" title you apply to them or they apply to themselves! This is equally true of those who might describe themselves as hard-line fundamentalists. People are people and people matter most, not ideologies.

The second caution looks in the other direction. Some assume all too readily that to espouse anything other than a fundamentalist stance towards the Bible means to devalue it. I am reminded that as a parent it is quite liberating to know that you are loved and respected even with your faults. Having a high regard for Scripture, including seeing it as the authority for faith and practice, does not demand that we deny the humanity of its writers. In fact, many have come to a deeper appreciation of Scripture when they have realized that it is precisely in these writings, which arose from real-life situations written by real-life human beings who are as human as we are, that we can find deep spiritual nourishment. Facing up to the realities of what these writings are in their context need not diminish respect for them. It becomes a matter of sorting out the wood from the trees, of finding and, for the Christian believer, of committing oneself to the God whose ways one finds enshrined in these documents of faith and experience. It is much more than following commands and always has been, but that was as hard for the contemporaries of Paul and Jesus to understand as it is for people today.

A Lot at Stake

People in those days dropped certain commands of Scripture not because they had grown tired of customs. The issue was more serious than that. They were deleting elements that people experienced as discriminatory and as posing obstacles to the work of God's love in the world. There was a lot at stake. They refused to transplant such demands into the new soil because they realized that to do so would be damaging. It makes me think of the eucalyptus trees. I could see no harm in their presence on the shores of Capernaum. But I know these fast-growing wonders of the wide red land have been found to impoverish the soils of many lands where they were used as a quick solution.

It would be tempting here for me to jump to some conclusions about what I think should or should not be transplanted from Scripture into current soil. There are two reasons why I do not want to do that. The first is that if I did so, you as the reader might be tempted to lay the book aside — and why not! After all, if the book's purpose is to argue for one particular application of these principles, for instance, about homosexuality, then that would be enough. Why read on? The rest of the book would amount to a very long footnote or appendix, of interest, perhaps, for people with spare time.

The second reason is that my purpose in this book is not to argue a particular case among the contemporary issues, but to invite people to step back from current discussion to consider what we can learn from Jesus and the gospels about approaches to Scripture. It is not that I want to withdraw from being engaged in contemporary issues; I *am* engaged in them and will continue to be so, but this is not the place. For I believe there are also some prior things that need sorting out, and one of them is our approach to Scripture. I am also aware that people who appreciate the rich and diverse approaches to Scripture found in the gospels will not necessarily reach the same conclusions as I do when it comes to dealing with contemporary issues. Some issues are in any case far from clear, and we are all in a process that necessarily entails critical questioning of our own conclusions. In that sense this study is open-ended. I invite readers to make their own connections and come to their own conclusions. In that sense each chapter will have a primarily historical focus. I will not be constantly calling the reader aside to reflect on wider connections, but will invite such contemplation in the conclusions of each chapter.

For those who wish to pursue the historical issues in greater detail I have appended a list of books, *For Further Reading,* at the end of the book. The present work arises out of the research that lay behind my major study, *Jesus' Attitude Towards the Law: A Study of the Gospels* (Grand Rapids: Eerdmans; earlier published in the series WUNT 2.97; Tübingen: Mohr Siebeck, 1997). I refer readers to the latter for detailed discussion, particularly of gospel passages and contemporary research. The present work is, however, different in orientation and method. It also includes some treatment of the historical Jesus and the traditions that existed before the gospels, though at the more general level appropriate for this work. Both reflect my concern to engage seriously with the gospels and the gospel, both as New Testament scholar and as follower of Christ.

In an earlier form the chapters of this book constituted lectures given at the Tasmanian Council of Churches School of Theology, in Hobart, in 1996. They have benefited from the interchange made possible there, as much as I also benefited from the warm fellowship of that gathering.

I cannot think about Jesus, and the Christian tradition I have come to love, without a sense of sand between my toes and grit in my sandals. I walk down that path to where the old synagogue had emerged from the excavations. Something happened here that really matters and that lives on. The bus was there to meet us for the return trip, and I had to leave it all behind. But something remains. This book is about what remains with us today across time and space and culture — and what now remains overlaid with the silt and dust of centuries on the shore of that ancient lake.

BEFORE MARK

People Matter Most, Not Laws

The account of Jesus' ministry in Mark's Gospel begins with a day in Capernaum. What may have been isolated anecdotes now forms a series of events which run from Mark 1:14-33. Jesus enlists four local fishermen for his cause (1:16-20), confronts a madman in the synagogue during a sabbath service (1:21-28), heals the mother-in-law of Simon Peter, one of the fishermen (1:29-31), and responds to the sick and needy brought to him after sunset (1:32-33). We do not know how Mark came to know of these stories, but they are typical of what we find elsewhere. Jesus is known as a healer, and he follows normal Jewish observance of the sabbath. Strict sabbath observance is probably the reason why people waited until sunset before carrying their needy to Jesus; for days were counted from sunset to sunset. After sunset it was no longer the sabbath day.

Jesus and the Leper

Jesus was a Jew at home in a Jewish setting. This finds confirmation in the anecdote about the leper which Mark introduces shortly afterwards (1:40-45). In it Jesus is obviously uncomfortable with the fact that the man has crashed through forbidden barriers in making his approach to Jesus. Lepers were to remain separate and cry, "Unclean,

unclean!" One set of ancient manuscripts even describes Jesus' response as one of direct anger. Even after the healing Jesus sends him off sternly to follow the instructions set down in the Scriptures: he should show himself to the priests and make the prescribed offering. Jesus' behavior was typical for an observant Jew of the time. The striking thing is that, challenged by such human need, Jesus went along with the man's plea. The story holds together a picture of Jesus as sharing traditional Jewish sensitivities on the basis of biblical law and a picture of a Jesus willing nevertheless to cross boundaries for the sake of human need.

Jesus and the Woman Who Was "Unclean"

We find two further anecdotes in Mark which portray Jesus in similar terms. Both concern women. One is found in 5:23-26. It concerns a woman suffering from internal hemorrhaging. According to biblical law it rendered her unclean and required that she remain separate. In an act of daring she moves through the crowd behind Jesus, believing that if she touches the tassel on his garment she will be healed. She succeeds. But then Jesus turns angrily, wanting to know who had touched him. As it stands, the story suggests Jesus sensed a flow of power from himself to the woman. That may well be, although it is equally likely that in its earlier versions the story told of Jesus' reaction to being touched by another person who was unclean. People telling the story in a Jewish context would have been well aware that such a woman was unclean and that this would have posed a problem for Jesus. It would have rendered him unclean. Despite his initial reaction he responds to the woman positively.

People who retold this story were celebrating Jesus' positive response to such a woman, whom others would have rejected. But at the same time it tells us something about Jesus' starting point in strict Judaism. The detail Matthew adds (9:20), but which Mark may already presuppose — that Jesus wore tassels — that is, fringes on his garment as a sign of respect for the commandments, reinforces this image (see also Mark 6:56). Numbers 15:37-40 instructs Israelite men to wear such fringes and some did, Jesus included.

Jesus and the Foreign Woman

The second story is even more shocking for the image it portrays of Jesus. Traveling into non-Jewish territory Jesus is confronted by a non-Jewish woman wanting help for her daughter (7:24-30). Jesus' initial response is gruff: it is not right to take the children's bread and throw it to the dogs. Even if he had household puppies in mind, the point is clear enough and highly offensive. It shows Jesus' starting point as one of a conservative Jew who takes very seriously the biblical distinction between Jew and non-Jew. But again, the story has been passed down because Jesus finally responded to the woman and her need. As the earlier story became a vehicle for celebrating the inclusion of women, so this story became a vehicle for celebrating the later inclusion of Gentiles in the Christian community.

Jesus and the Army Commander

A similar story is found in the source material that Matthew and Luke share, which we call Q. It tells of a Gentile army commander who approached Jesus in Capernaum, seeking help for his sick servant (Q 7:1-4, 6-9; cf. Luke 7:1-10; Matt. 8:5-13; on Q see Chapter 3). Matthew records the version of Jesus' response which has best claim to being earliest: "Am I to come and heal him?" (8:7). In other words, Jesus is again showing reluctance. Why? The issue becomes obvious when we hear the commander's response. "I am not worthy to have you come under my roof." In saying this he was addressing the problem head-on. He assumes that as a strict, observant Jew Jesus would avoid entering the house of a Gentile. Luke tells us that Peter had the same initial qualms about responding to the army commander, Cornelius, in the early days of the church (Acts 10-11). Yet, as with the leper, the woman with the hemorrhaging and the non-Jewish woman, Jesus shows he is prepared to cross the boundary. He still does not enter the Gentile's house; but he answers the commander's request and responds to his need.

Behind these stories is an image of Jesus as a fairly conservative Jew concerned to keep the biblical commandments relating to purity and boundaries, yet prepared to cross the boundaries in emergencies. It was the boundary crossing which began to mark him out and which came to be identified with his chief concerns. These come to the fore especially in a series of anecdotes Mark has incorporated in his gospel, in which Jesus is in dispute over interpretation of Scripture.

Who Can Declare God's Forgiveness of Sins?

One is the famous story of the paralyzed man let down through the roof of a house. It is now found in Mark 2:1-12. In its earliest form the story probably recounted a controversy that arose after Jesus told the man his sins were forgiven. Religious teachers object to Jesus' words. They are on shaky ground. Their objection will have been that Jesus claims he can declare to people that God forgives them. That would be normally for a priest to declare; at least, that was the usual practice. But there were no grounds in biblical law for such a restriction. The same problem appears to have arisen with John the Baptist, who declared people's sins forgiven when they repented and submitted to baptism.

Jesus' response to the objection is clever: "What is easier," he replies, "to say, 'Your sins are forgiven' or to say, 'Arise, take up your bed and walk'?" The answer all depends. At one level it is much easier to declare forgiveness than it is to tell someone who is lame to get up and walk. At another level declaring forgiveness is something they think should be forbidden to Jesus. Clearly Jesus puts both on the same level. What puts them on the same level? They are both acts of caring for the person. Now that is interesting because once again we see caring for people overriding all other concerns. In its present form we can see that Mark has woven the story into his narrative and related it to the themes he is developing. One is that Jesus is the Son of Man who has authority to forgive sins. Another is that he faces here and at his trial the charge of blasphemy. But at base the story is not really about blasphemy or about Jesus' claiming independent authority. It is about Jesus' claiming the right and authority to respond to human need as God's chief concern and defining his own role in these terms.

Bad Company

Mark includes a second story in 2:15-17. Behind it is an occasion in which strict interpreters of the Law raise a question mark over the fact that Jesus dines with toll collectors and other disreputable people. We know that this was a complaint raised more than once about Jesus. Why did someone claiming to teach about God's will ignore the wisdom of such passages as the first Psalm, which advised people to stay away from bad company? It was not that Jesus was directly breaking a commandment, but the behavior was unbecoming and inappropriate. It might have been even more serious than that. Jesus' critics probably considered such people as unclean as well as immoral, or at least as very likely to ignore biblical laws about purity and tithing with regard to food and its preparation. Jesus' response is another short quip: "The sick need a doctor, not the well." By the time the story came to Mark someone had added more to this, so that Jesus went on to explain: "I did not come to call the righteous but sinners." Matthew adds even more and puts in before this a challenge given by Jesus to: "Go and learn what this means: I desire mercy and not sacrifice" (9:13). Matthew's interpretation is on the mark. Originally Jesus said it all with one short quip. The point is that Jesus explains his presence among these people as an expression of concern for them. That matters more than other considerations, such as keeping bad company or mixing with people who were unclean.

The Sabbath Was Made for People,
Not People for the Sabbath

These are not stories about Jesus being reluctant as were the first set of stories. But they share with those stories a common thread: what ultimately mattered was people and responding to their need. Mark shows that Jesus treated sabbath law the same way. Behind Mark 3:1-6 is a memory that Jesus healed a man with a shriveled hand in the synagogue on the sabbath day. Again he faced criticism. Again he answered with a brief quip: "Is it lawful to do good on the sabbath or to do harm?" It must have infuriated his critics because it did not answer their complaint, at least, not directly. What it said was that responding to people's need took priority over all else. This answer has also been expanded, perhaps by Mark himself, with the words, "to save life or to kill?" This heightens the drama of Mark's narrative, because he makes the episode end with the critics plotting to kill — to kill Jesus. This is part of the way Mark linked such incidents with what later happened to Jesus: his arrest, trial, and crucifixion.

Our focus is the stories as they existed before Mark wove them into his gospel, and especially what they may tell us about Jesus. One more sabbath incident deserves our attention. It is found in Mark 2:23-28. In its earliest form it seems to be another case of complaints against Jesus. This time he and his disciples were walking in the grain fields on the sabbath, picking the grain and eating it. They were hardly harvesting! It seems they were doing no more than idly plucking single heads, rolling out the seed and eating it. But for very extreme interpreters this constituted work on the sabbath and so broke the biblical command. Jesus' original response is probably found in 2:27, a typically clever response characteristic of Jesus: "The sabbath was made for people, not people for the sabbath." Initially it was not an argument about hungry people feeding themselves, but about how silly it was to be finicky in such matters. Such bother about detail overlooked the very purpose of the sabbath, which was not to restrict people but to benefit them. Again, Jesus put people first, not the details of rules.

This story, too, has received some expansions. Someone put in the reference to David and his hungry men. This shifted the focus to human need and naturally leads us to think the disciples were very hungry. It is not a very successful illustration. Its author gives the wrong name for the priest involved. Abiathar was not high priest in the time of David; it was Ahimelech (1 Sam. 21:1-7). Still, it did bring out what was a genuine concern of Jesus as we have seen: concern for human need. As in 2:10, so 2:28 speaks of Jesus as the Son of Man, a figure of great authority, and declares that this authority includes what should be done on the sabbath. But behind all of this is Jesus' clever quip which said it so simply: people matter most to God, not commandments.

What Mattered to Jesus

It is time to review our findings. None of these accusations against Jesus had sufficient warrant in the Scripture. Only very extreme, very literal interpretation could claim that Jesus broke biblical law. As we saw in the earlier stories, Jesus' starting point was one of complete faithfulness to the biblical laws. But his approach to Scripture was different from his antagonists. He understood it as teaching that God was concerned first and foremost for people. This was the overriding rule that made sense of the rest. Behind it is a different understanding of God from theirs. Their understanding of God pictured God as someone primarily concerned with his commandments and rules; Jesus' understanding of God was that God was primarily concerned with the good of people, and that commandments and laws were subordinate to that. It is important to recognize this difference, because it runs through much of what Jesus said and did. It did not mean that Jesus spurned the commandments, let alone the Scriptures. On the contrary he took them very seriously; it was a question of how he did so.

Matthew was right in linking the approach of Jesus to the approach expressed in Hosea 6:6, where the prophet proclaims God's approach: "I desire mercy and not sacrifice" (9:13; 12:7). This was not an attack on sacrifices. It was, after all, the temple authorities responsible for the temple system with its sacrifices who preserved his writing as holy Scripture. It was rather a typically inclusive contrast which meant: to show compassion is more important than to offer sacrifices. Jesus belonged with those Jews of the time who were strongly in touch with the prophetic heritage and who had learned from the psalms that God's mercy and compassion endures forever.

A Matter of Priorities: Inside and Outside

We find a similar kind of contrast in another of Jesus' quips made in a situation of controversy. Behind Mark 7:1-23 is an incident in which devout religious people complain about Jesus' disciples (and probably also Jesus himself, originally). They ate food without first washing their hands to make them ritually clean. Again we are dealing with a very extreme group and a practice that is very hard to justify on the basis of scriptural law, but doubtless seen by them as an implication of what Scripture demanded.

The episode now forms part of an extensive controversy. The earlier form probably simply told of the complaint and then had Jesus say something like: "It is not what enters a person that makes them unclean, but what comes out of them." This clever quip was doubtless not an attack on the biblical food laws; it was an attempt to change the focus of attention. It employs a kind of basic humor: at a literal level we could rephrase it: it's what comes out of a person that stinks, not what enters them! At a deeper level it is saying: what should really concern us is what goes on inside people that produces immoral and destructive behavior. This deserves more attention than observance of food laws and associated purity issues. Jesus doubtless kept such observances; concerns about purity affected his initial response to lepers and women and non-Jews; but he objected to the finicky extension of such observances being promoted by these extreme groups. There were things that mattered more. Attitudes and behaviors that are caring and not destructive matter more than detailed observances.

Look to God's Intention

Another of Jesus' famous quips is: "What God has joined together let no human being rend apart!" (Mark 10:9). Originally it seems to have stood on its own as Jesus' response to detailed arguments about what might qualify as grounds for men to divorce their wives (biblical law has no provision for women to divorce their husbands). Jesus' response turns the attention away from preoccupation with details of the Law to the foundation principles that should lie behind it. It uses imagery cleverly, as do many of Jesus' short quips. If God has joined two together, what on earth are you doing trying to pull them apart! That throws an entirely different light on divorce. It may not have been intended to forbid divorce altogether, but rather to challenge people to take the whole matter much more seriously. It is not a matter of how we can get around a law, but how do we come to terms creatively with what is a failure. Be that as it may, over time the story has been expanded. As with the story about Jesus and his disciples in the grain fields, so here Jesus' quip has been supplemented with verses from Scripture. The effect is to change the character of Jesus' quip from a single powerfully evocative challenge to a summary at the end of Scripture quotations.

Keeping the Rules and Missing the Point

The issue in all of this was not that ethical commandments of Scriptures carried more weight than commandments relating to ritual purity or food or sacrifices. To some degree this was true. But Jesus was not playing off one set of commandments against another. Rather he was contrasting a way of interpreting Scripture and responding to its message with an approach that put all the emphasis on literal fulfillment. This comes out dramatically in Jesus' encounter with the rich man who asked him about eternal life (Mark 10:17-22). Jesus is serious when, in response, he refers to the ten commandments, especially those that concern fellow human beings. When the man answers that he has been keeping these Jesus loves him; the man had genuinely started in the right place. By challenging him to give up his possessions and distribute the proceeds to the poor, Jesus exposes what was missing in the man's approach. The man had focused on keeping commandments, but had missed the point of the whole exercise even though he may have kept them without wavering. The point of the commandments is to do God's will, to live a life of caring and compassion. It is not to follow instructions, to keep someone's rules.

The trouble with that sort of approach is that it assumes God is a selfish being who wants everyone to love and obey him for his own sake, instead of recognizing that God is loving and generous and wants us to be engaged in loving and generosity with each other. If you love a God who is loving, you become loving; if you love a God who is portrayed as loving only himself and his laws, then you lose touch with loving. Jesus' mention of concern for the poor exposed the flaw in the man's spirituality. Jesus invited him to follow. It was not that the man had been on the wrong track and should now replace the commandments by loyalty to Jesus. On the contrary, he should follow the commands of Scripture because they are the way to eternal life, but he should do so with a totally different attitude: the attitude espoused by Jesus.

We find a similar approach coming through when a sympathetic Jewish teacher asks Jesus about the greatest commandment (12:28-34). It is a rare example of something like consensus. Both agree that loving God with one's whole being and loving one's neighbor as oneself is at the heart of Scripture's demand. This matters more than anything else. The man's words recall the words of Hosea about mercy mattering more than sacrifices.

Doing God's Will Is More Than Keeping Commands

Jesus was at home within his religion, the religion of Judaism; but he was not at home with some of his fellow Jews. Jesus was an observant Jew. It is hard to find a single instance where Jesus could be legitimately accused of contravening the Law as set out in Scripture. Even the sayings that Matthew has turned into sharp contrasts: "You have heard it said, but I say" (5:21-48), are not an attack on the Law but an affirmation of its claim at a stricter, deeper level. He outlaws not only murder but murderous attitudes; not only adultery but adulterous attitudes. He permits no exception on divorce. He outlaws oaths altogether. He forbids retaliation and enjoins love for one's neighbor.

We shall return to these sayings when considering Matthew's gospel; but behind all of these teachings is a concern to give attention to what is at the heart of the Law's demands. Forbidding oaths was not about adding stricter rules but addressing the underlying problems oaths were meant to address: honest rather than manipulative speech. Similarly, forbidding divorce was not about imposing harsh strictures but about countering exploitation of women. Of course, those who approached the biblical statements at a strictly literal level could argue that Jesus' statements contradicted the scriptural provision for divorce and for oaths and charge him with undermining Scripture. But they can only do so when they approach Scripture in such a literalistic way. Yet it has also been common to look back at Jesus' words from the same literalist perspective and to claim that he was deliberately setting himself against the Law. This misunderstands Jesus and his place in his own religion.

Conflicts and Crucifixion

One of the problems lies with the way Mark has woven his various traditions together. After the group of stories in 2:1–3:6, which tell of Jesus' facing accusations that he broke the Law, Mark adds that the accusers, whom he named Pharisees, formed an alliance with the Herodians, sympathizers with Herod Antipas's government, to have Jesus put to death. He goes on to mention religious authorities who came from Jerusalem to confront Jesus. In this way Mark paints opposition to Jesus as a semi-official exercise that finally brought him to court before the high priest and to crucifixion.

It is difficult to determine how much this corresponds to historical reality and how much it is Mark's reconstruction of events from a time when Christians were beginning to be pursued at a more formal level. The problem is that the accusations laid against Jesus appear to represent extremist positions. None of them reappears in the account of Jesus' trial. In fact the charge that Jesus advocated breaking the Law is strikingly absent, even from Mark's account of Jesus' trial. Mark seems to have oversimplified the events in the light of later experience; his own sources on the trial and death of Jesus, which were doubtless very early, do not support his case. Nevertheless it is quite possible that such controversies became known and very probable that Jesus was seen as a figure of controversy and that this contributed to the fear that he was a source of unrest in the community.

Jesus — a Cause of Unrest in an Unstable Region

It was this latter concern that played a significant role in Jesus' arrest, trial, and execution. It is reflected behind the account in John's gospel of Caiaphas arguing that it was better to have Jesus executed than run the risk of the Romans imposing harsher measures of control because of the unrest Jesus caused (11:47-53). This was very realistic. The Romans were concerned about stability on the eastern flank of the empire, and Judea was notoriously unstable. Any person outside the normal power structures who commanded a popular following was suspect. This accounts for the charge against Jesus that he was wanting to be a Messiah, that is, an Anointed liberator of his people. The Romans knew what to do with so-called liberators, and they clearly treated Jesus as belonging in this general category. They mocked him as a would-be king with a robe and crown; they executed him between two other revolutionary brigands; they offered to swap Jesus for the guerrilla leader, Barabbas; they identified the charge against Jesus as "the king of the Jews." The Jewish authorities of the time had pressed their case successfully before Pilate. Yet nothing in the accounts of Jesus' ministry supports the charge that he was a revolutionary of this kind.

Also, the fact that his disciples were not immediately rounded up and executed along with him indicates that the issue was tied more to his individual actions.

The Charges Against Jesus

From the various accounts given in the gospels we may never know what really went on in those last days. Did Jesus claim to be the Messiah in a different sense, and was this misunderstood? Mark's account of the trial speaks of two charges (14:55-64). The charge that turns the tide is that of blasphemy (14:61-64). The problem here is that nothing we know of either the Old Testament or later Jewish tradition appears to justify the charge. It seems wrong. No one else who claimed to be God's anointed, "the Christ, the son of the Blessed," assuming Jesus agreed that he was, was charged with being blasphemous. John's gospel may shed further light on this, because it has the issues of the trial spread through Jesus' ministry. Jesus' opponents consistently misinterpret his statements that he is God's Son as implying some kind of literal equality with God (e.g., 5:16-20; 10:31-39). This, Jesus consistently rejects, preferring to speak of a oneness with God that consisted in his obedience to God's will.

In other words, Mark's account of Jesus' trial before the Jewish high priest, like John's account of the charges made during his ministry, may well reflect charges later made against Christians when they proclaimed Jesus as the Messiah and Son of God. The charge then and the charge at Jesus' trial, if it was historical, was false. But it provided the stuff for an accusation before Pilate which would stick: Jesus was a troublemaker, in the Messiah-liberator mold.

Jesus and the Temple

The other accusation in Mark's account of Jesus' trial enlightens us further. Mark tells us straight out that it was false. The accusers report that

Jesus declared that he would destroy the temple and raise it again in three days (14:58). Jesus had, in fact, predicted the destruction of the temple according to Mark 13, but he had not said that he, himself, would destroy or rebuild it. Thus, while the charge is false, it carried some substance: Jesus had spoken against the temple. That would rile both the temple-based authorities, because it attacked their integrity, and the Romans because they guaranteed the temple's security.

Jesus' attack on the temple also features in the incident where he came into the outer courtyard and caused a disturbance among the moneychangers and those who sold birds and animals for sacrifice (Mark 11:15-17; John 2:14-17). In Mark we read that Jesus strung together two statements from the prophets and declared God's will: "My house shall be called a house of prayer for all people; but you have made it a den of robbers." Whether or not Jesus actually said these words, they offer a fair indication of Jesus' stance. Jesus was not attacking the temple as such; he honored it as God's house. He was attacking malpractice. The malpractice probably had less to do with any overcharging that might have been going on and more to do with the way commercial concerns were intruding in what was meant to be holy space.

Elsewhere, too, Jesus attacked such abuses on the part of the religious leadership. Even the parable of the Good Samaritan (Luke 10:30-37) is an indirect attack on the skewed sense of priorities of people connected with the temple. Such an approach would not endear Jesus to the authorities, who at worst were bent on preserving their own interests, and at best were concerned that nothing undermine the continued existence of the temple and its worship.

Jesus Did Not Reject the Law or the Scriptures

When, in Chapter 3, we consider the information preserved in Q, we shall return to this theme because it sheds significant light on what Jesus criticized in the context of his own religion. One thing is clear: neither Jesus' trial nor his attitude towards the temple suggests that he rejected biblical law. The issues were about abuse of the Law, and the accusations were based on misunderstanding. We must assume that Jesus lived and behaved in accordance with the demands of scriptural law. He would have paid the tithe (rendering to God the things that are God's [Mark 12:17]). He would have observed purity laws with regard to food and drink; he would have purified himself after encounters with corpses or other situations declared unclean. Otherwise we would surely hear of it. Some have cited his words to a would-be disciple that he let the dead bury the dead (Q 9:60; Luke 9:60; Matt. 8:22) as a harsh rejection of biblical injunctions about respect for parents and responsibility for the dead, but nothing indicates that it was seen in this way at the time.

Apparently Jesus followed the biblical injunction of wearing tassels on his garments to symbolize his commitment to God's Law. We find him under attack with regard to Law observance only from extremists. Jesus belonged within Judaism; he celebrated its festivals and its Passover, he worshiped in its synagogues, and he made pilgrimage to the temple, which he called God's house. He even became so concerned for the temple that he attacked its financial dealers and their distortion of the temple's purpose. Among and within his people Jesus reaffirmed God's radical love and made his belief in this God the basis for his interpretation of Scripture and for the living out of his religion. There is much more to be said here, but it will have to wait until we discuss the other major source for the gospel story, the material called Q and the traditions found outside of Mark.

Solidly Jewish

Even by mainly considering the anecdotes preserved in Mark and those closely related we have been able to glimpse something of Jesus' attitude towards the faith of his people. He was solidly Jewish. He observed the laws and provisions set out in Scripture. But he approached his Bible on the basis of a theology that understood God as loving and generous. On this basis Jesus was able to set priorities that affected the way he applied Scripture to everyday life. In this, people mattered most, not rules and commandments. The rules were subordinate to God's overriding compassion for people, and they were designed to express this. People mattered most, because for Jesus people mattered most for God. This did not lead Jesus to set Scripture or its commandments aside. It enabled him to set them in perspective. It meant that on the one hand he expounded God's will in a way that went far beyond the commandments, as in the case of his sayings about murder and adultery. It meant, on the other hand, that he rejected the fundamentalism of his day, which was obsessed with literal fulfillment and approached the Scriptures with a theology of a God preoccupied, like the worst kind of self-indulgent tyrant, with having everything center on himself.

Why Jesus Was Not a Fundamentalist: He Centered on God and God's Reign

Why did Jesus approach the Scriptures in this way? Part of the answer lies, I believe, in the way he appears to have centered his thought, at least as it is reflected in his sayings. Mark summarizes Jesus' message of good news as a message about the coming of the kingdom of God, God's reign (1:14-15). We shall return to the image of God's reign in more detail when discussing the material found in Q. For the present I want to observe that when you make some single theme or symbol the focus of your thought, it has the effect of setting everything else in perspective. The kingdom of God mattered most; all else is subordinate to this. It becomes therefore the basis for a new way of looking at Scripture and its commands. Of course, a term like the kingdom of God lends itself very well to this process. The kingdom of God means God's reign. It puts God and God's will at the center.

Jesus' Vision

But it is more than just that Jesus centered on God's will. After all, those who wanted to keep every command meticulously could also appeal to their desire to do God's will. In Jesus' day the reign of God was something to which people looked forward in hope. In Jesus' way of handling it, this hope encompassed a change in the whole of society; it would be a time of blessing for the poor and hungry, for the depressed and downtrodden. It would be a time of restoration and renewal of God's people. While Jesus would have thought in terms of renewal of Israel, he probably also envisaged that this would include blessing for all the nations. Often Jesus used the image of the banquet to describe this great gathering of wholeness and peace. In sharing this vision Jesus stands within the stream of the prophets who spoke in similar terms of hope for the future. "Your kingdom come!" was to be the cry of Jesus' followers.

Having such a hope affects one's priorities at a very obvious level in the present. It sets values. You cannot long for fulfillment of such a vision and not want to see it happening in the present. You cannot proclaim good news to the poor and inclusion of the outcast and sinner and not start applying such inclusiveness in the present. So both the fact of having a focus of hope and the content of that hope have an impact on the way you interpret life in the present; and it includes the way you interpret the Scriptures. When we think back to those stories where Jesus was in conflict with his accusers, we can see that the priorities determining Jesus' interpretation were directly related to his vision of God's reign in the future. For, just as in the coming kingdom people matter most as God's compassion is poured out, so in the present, in interpreting God's will, people matter most and compassion is to the fore.

What Mattered Most and
What Mattered Least in Interpreting Scripture

Another important factor in sustaining Jesus' approach to interpreting the Scripture and its laws is when loyalty to Jesus himself becomes a point of focus. As this developed, it became easier to develop a set of perspectives about what mattered most and what mattered least in interpreting Scripture. We shall see this in the chapters that follow.

These two different attitudes towards Scripture and the theologies they represent are alive and well in our own time. In the one there is no flexibility. The Bible's commandments are eternally valid and unchanging. They must be obeyed because God has given them and God as the highest authority is to be obeyed without question. God wants such obedience for himself to the smallest detail. By contrast, there is the approach closer to that of Jesus, which makes God and God's compassion central. The biblical commandments are expressions of God's will as perceived by the people of Israel and the people of the New Testament. They belong within and in subordination to God's eternal unchanging love and compassion, which sometimes go far beyond them and in doing so sometimes depart from their literal demand. The one approach sets store on the letter. The other sets store on the spirit of what is written. The one puts what is written at the heart of things; the other puts God at the heart of things. For one, laws matter most, because they matter most to God; for the other, people matter most because they matter most to God. One brings death; the other brings life.

Yet despite these fundamental differences of approach, both these extremists and Jesus remain within the one faith of Israel. Beside them are many others of varying degrees of strictness. Jesus was not alone in his approach. Other Jews before him had espoused such a direction. His attitude was itself thoroughly based in Scripture, especially in the early prophets. But the same was true of his critics. They, too, could claim strong biblical warrant. The same Scripture spawned a diversity of interpretive approaches. The source of their inspiration, itself inspired, inspired conflicting approaches and still does. In the end the appeal to Scripture needed something else; but that was yet to come.

The conflicts *of* Jesus became conflicts *about* Jesus and laid the basis for new and radical steps towards a resolution that would stretch Israel's faith to the breaking point. The following chapters observe this conflict at various stages and in various forms as the gospel writers reassess and redefine Jesus' attitude towards his own religion as part of their search for a more satisfactory basis of authority and a more satisfactory basis for interpreting the Scriptures.

• 2 •

MARK

Dispensing with Externals

Mark appears to have been the first to draw together the various sayings and anecdotes of Jesus into a single account of Jesus' ministry. I say, Jesus' ministry, because, in fact, Mark's account covers only the period from Jesus' baptism to his death and resurrection, barely a year of Jesus' life. Nevertheless it is a powerful portrait and formed the basis for the gospels of Matthew and Luke, who later revised and expanded it. Mark is looking back over forty years to Jesus' ministry. Much has gone on in the intervening four decades. Mark writes in a predominantly non-Jewish context; at least, he assumes that Gentiles are an established part of his community, although he also assumes that his hearers, whether Gentiles or Jews, have a sufficient knowledge of the Old Testament to pick up the occasional allusive reference.

The Authority of Jesus and the Authority of Scripture

For Mark, Jesus is the supreme authority. About this there is no question. So the issue of the authority of Scripture and its interpretation must be seen in this light. Theoretically there were a number of options about the way the two authorities, that of Jesus and that of Scripture, might be seen to relate to one another. One is that Jesus should be seen as a further authority, beside the authority of Scripture, and coming as the climax of God's acts of revelation; both the Scriptures and Jesus are absolute authority and both are in complete harmony and remain in force. Another is that Jesus replaces the authority of Scripture, which now takes second place or may even be disregarded altogether. A third is that the coming of Jesus effects some revisions of Scripture commandments, but that with these exceptions both Jesus and the Scriptures remain supreme authority. The exceptions might be few or many. Each of these options had its following in the early church and will be found in the gospels considered in this book.

It is clear that for Mark the Scriptures still have authority. He cites them from the very beginning in hailing John's appearance as fulfillment of prophecy. Fulfillment of scriptural predictions and echoes of biblical stories are a constant feature in Mark's narrative. At Jesus' baptism the words from on high, "You are my beloved son with whom I am well pleased," (1:11) echo the words of Psalm 2:7, "You are my son; today I have given birth to you" and Isaiah 42:1, "You are my servant with whom I am well pleased." They may also allude to Isaac as Abraham's "beloved son" (Gen. 22). It is not unusual that a range of allusions may be present in a single incident or saying, as here. We find the same in the feeding of the five thousand (6:32-44). It contains echoes not only of the manna in the wilderness, but also of Elisha's feeding miracle (2 Kings 5:42-44). In the same way the story of the stilling of the storm (4:35-41) echoes the story of Jonah and of the psalms, which employed the imagery of storms at sea (Jon. 1:4-16; Ps. 65:7; 89:9; 107:25-32). The effect of all these allusions is to reinforce the sense that the story Mark is telling has the same kind of quality. It is sacred story, like the stories of old. Whether with such allusions or in direct quotation, Mark appeals to the Scriptures as authority.

Jesus' Authority Takes Center Stage

The authority who takes the center stage in Mark, however, is Jesus himself. Mark contrasts his authority in teaching with that of the scribes (1:21-22). Mark connects Jesus' teaching authority with his authority to deal with demonic powers (1:21-28). It is the same power, Mark argues, which is coming through in Jesus' words. Mark had laid the foundation for this understanding by his account of Jesus' baptism. Jesus has a special relationship with God as God's son, and God has given him the Holy Spirit through which he can do what he does.

In the early chapters of his gospel Mark builds up the image of Jesus and his authority. By chapter 5 he has brought the account of Jesus' miraculous powers to a climax with the stilling of the storm (4:35-41) and the showdown with the legion of demons at Gerasa (5:1-20). However legendary such anecdotes may be in their origins, they now serve to make a powerful point. Jesus has supreme authority. This authority belongs for Mark inextricably with Jesus' authority as a teacher. The miracle of the stilling of the storm follows directly after a series of parables in which Jesus uses the image of the miracle of the harvest (4:1-34). From the vulnerable seed sown in the soil comes a miraculous bounty, and that, despite the losses along the way. For Mark, the seed is Jesus' teaching.

The Authority to Forgive

In the previous chapter we already noted the stories of conflict in 2:1–3:6. There, too, the theme is authority. In Mark's version of the anecdote of the paralyzed man let down through the roof Jesus' final words are: "The Son of Man has authority on earth to forgive sins" (2:10). If in the earlier versions of the story the argument was that declaring God's forgiveness should not be made the right of a few, now the focus is on Jesus as the one who carries such authority. Similarly, Mark's version of the conflict in the grain fields ends now with Jesus' declaration that "The Son of Man is lord even of the Sabbath" (2:28). This comes close to claiming not only that he has authority to interpret sabbath law, but also that the sabbath is at his disposal. That is probably not Mark's intention at this point, although as we shall see, it is the view of the writer of the fourth gospel.

The middle of the five stories in 2:1–3:6 now reads as a conflict over fasting between Jesus, on the one hand, and disciples of John the Baptist and the Pharisees, on the other (2:18-22). Originally the incident reflects the problem of the different lifestyles of Jesus and John with Jesus' quip: "Surely the people of the bridal party can't be mournful while the bridegroom is with them!" This reflects the fact that John was austere and ascetic, adopting the stance that the good was yet to come, whereas Jesus believed that the good was already becoming reality. Hence his celebratory lifestyle which attracted criticism. We have another case of a story that underwent considerable development.

Old and New Teaching about Scripture

Attached to it now are two sayings that contrast the old and the new: don't sew old patches onto new garments and don't pour new wine into old wineskins! (2:21-22). They are not advocating that people throw old garments or old wine away; but they are highlighting tensions between the old and the new. Jesus' quip also invited the further reflection that he himself might be thought of as the bridegroom and his death as the departure of the bridegroom (2:19b-20). You can see how the original anecdote had begun to expand in various directions as people exploited its potential for further meaning. This was typical of the process that had been going on. To return to Mark, it is clear that the story underlines Jesus' new authority and hints at tensions with the old which, in Mark's ongoing account, will indeed lead to his death.

Within the five stories contained in 2:1–3:6 Mark is underlining Jesus' authority when it comes to determining what is God's will, and that includes applying Scripture commands. But the focus is more on the person of Jesus because of who he is than on the interpretation as such. He is the new authority. His opponents are not now being confronted only with an argument about how scriptural authority should be applied; they are facing a new claim to authority. Yet this new authority is not acting arbitrarily, as if scriptural authority did not matter. The emphases of the original anecdotes still come through. The new authority is characterized by a concern for people more than laws: people matter most.

An Unauthorized Authority

The scene is now set for further confrontations. The first comes in Mark 3:22-30, where authorities from Jerusalem accuse Jesus of deriving his power from demonic forces. The elaborate temple system based on the instructions found in Scripture was the primary channel of ministry within Israel. By it Israel's faith was sustained and nurtured. It provided the words, symbols, and activities that together gave expression to Israel's faith. It had always been difficult to accommodate additional channels of grace or divine power. At times it was difficult to find a place for more unorthodox prophets. John the Baptist posed a problem. Jesus was in the same category; what Mark records here doubtless reflects a historical reality during Jesus' ministry. It is a neat solution to categorize people out of contention. Mark shows Jesus flatly rejecting the accusation and responding with dire warnings of his own. In Mark's view, the truth was that Jesus represented God's authority; to reject Jesus was to reject God. He has Jesus say as much in 8:38: "Whoever is ashamed of me in this adulterous and sinful generation, of him will the Son of Man be ashamed when he comes in the glory of his Father with the holy angels."

Free from Family Systems

It is interesting to note that Mark has set this episode within another story that may have meant a lot more to his hearers. Jesus' own people fear he is mad and try to bring him home (3:20-21). Confronted by their efforts, Jesus declares that his true family consists of those who commit themselves to doing God's will (3:31-35). The approach is typical of Jesus, as we shall see again when looking at material preserved in Q. God's will overrides all other priorities. The fact that Jesus' own family puts a counterclaim, however misinformed, is particularly shocking. It coheres well with the shock tactics Mark employs elsewhere, especially in portraying Jesus' disciples as having almost no grasp of what he was about and behaving in ways that were contrary to his values.

Mark's Skill Contrasts Two Kinds of Spiritual Food

The next time Jesus confronts authorities from Jerusalem is 7:1-23. We have already noted that it is an extensively expanded version of an anecdote in which Jesus responded to criticism about failure to wash hands ritually before meals with another clever quip: what comes out of a person is the problem; not so much what goes into them. Mark has made the expanded version the centerpiece of a careful composition that deserves our special attention. Basically it runs from 6:7 to 8:21, but it is also carefully connected with what precedes and what follows. To put it simply, Mark has used the image of food to contrast the teaching of Jesus with that of the Pharisees. The teaching of Jesus makes room for both Jew and Gentile without discrimination. The teaching of the Pharisees does not. That is Mark's argument and, as we shall see, it has important implications for understanding the way Mark handles the Scriptures.

Mark's Jesus Eliminates Discrimination

Mark uses 7:1-23 as the basis for what he is saying about Jesus' teaching. He even summarizes the point of the passage in a few words in 7:19 to the effect that in all this Jesus was "declaring all foods clean." The issue of "clean" and "unclean" was about more than foods, and it is clear that Mark understands Jesus to be declaring such distinctions invalid. This is important because such distinctions were the basis for discrimination against Gentiles. If they are dropped, Gentiles can be included on the same basis as Jews. Mark is not inventing something here. He is reflecting on the resolution to a major conflict with which the early church grappled and which is reflected in Paul's letters and indirectly in Acts. Obviously Mark's community was based on a solution close to what Paul had advocated and what is reflected also in Ephesians.

If 7:1-23 represents for Mark Jesus' rejection of such distinctions, 7:24-30, Jesus' encounter with the Syrophoenician woman, reflects the implications of this teaching. We have seen that it is an anecdote which begins with a conservative Jesus reluctant to respond to a Gentile, quite striking in its discriminatory terms (children and dogs). But it ends with Jesus crossing the boundary and responding to the woman's need. The story has been told and retold to celebrate this crossing and that is its function in Mark.

Mark and the Feeding Miracles

When we move outwards from the centerpiece, 7:1-23 and 7:24-30, we find on either side the two great feeding miracles, the feeding of the five thousand (6:32-44) and the feeding of the four thousand (8:1-10). The feeding of the five thousand takes place in Jewish territory. It uses imagery strongly reminiscent of Israel. This is not only so in the echo of the manna in the wilderness, which it shares with the feeding of the four thousand. It is also present in the comment, "For they were like sheep without a shepherd," echoing the description of Israel in Numbers 27:17 and elsewhere; in the fact that the people are to be seated in groups of hundreds and fifties like Israel in the wilderness; and in the figure of twelve baskets of leftovers, echoing the twelve tribes of Israel. By contrast the feeding of the four thousand, which is otherwise almost a mirror image of the first feeding, has none of these features and takes place in Gentile territory. Here there are seven baskets. The first feeding, of the five thousand, and the stories that surround it, take place in Jewish territory; the second feeding, of the four thousand, and the narratives that surround it, take place in Gentile territory. The symbolism is obvious: there is food for both Jew and Gentile. Both Jew and Gentile have been included without discrimination. That food includes the teaching about compassion, which is there for all and which removes unnecessary barriers.

Beware of Food Poisoning!

Mark makes the additional effort to underline what he is driving at by leading the hearer to reflect on it again in 8:16-21. Here Jesus interviews his disciples, who offer shockingly bad models of comprehension. The message is: "Beware of the leaven (food) of the Pharisees and Herodians!" Mentioning the Herodians recalls 3:6, where they were featured with the Pharisees in wanting to kill Jesus. And at the beginning of the composition the Herodian Antipas had John beheaded at his birthday banquet! (6:21-31). This is dark humor. Mark is making the point that at stake here is life or death, as he sees it. Jesus continues the discussion by drawing the disciples' attention to the numbers of baskets at the feedings (8:19-21). That should enable them to put two and two together, so to speak. Mark is also encouraging those who listen to his gospels to grasp the symbolism. Twelve was a standard allusion to Israel and seven to the universe as a whole — more commonly, seventy or seventy-two as the number of nations on earth according to biblical tradition. Mark is making a strong statement about the inclusion that has taken place and declaring that the teaching which made it possible is life and nourishment of all peoples. It is a brilliant composition that makes the point forcibly.

Mark's Jesus Attacks Preoccupation with Externals

It is now time to examine the centerpiece more closely, because it has major implications for understanding Mark's approach to Scripture. Mark begins by describing the scene. The disciples eat bread without first ritually washing their hands (7:1-2). Pharisees and scribes from Jerusalem object. Mark explains to the hearers of his gospel that the

Pharisees and all Jews practiced such ritual washing before meals. This was obviously Mark's view, even though as a claim it has little support from the literature of the time and is probably wrong. Mark then adds a note about other ritual washings done to cups and plates and bronze vessels and beds (7:3-4). Considered in the broader context Mark's scorn of such practices is hard to miss. For Mark they belong at the level of irrelevant preoccupations, like the concern about the ritual washing of hands. They derive from the "tradition of the elders," in other words, instructions about purity passed down by Jewish teachers.

Mark makes it clear that Jesus rejects such practices and immediately links preoccupation with such externals to neglect of what really matters. That amounts to hypocrisy. The Pharisees believe they are doing God's will in following such elaborations, but it leads them instead to neglect God's commands (7:6-8). In 7:9-12 Jesus cites the practice of dedicating possessions to God as a way of claiming exemption from having to share them with needy parents. These kinds of innovations subvert rather than extend God's will in the world.

Mark's Jesus Rejects Bible Teaching on Food and Purity

So far the attack seems to be on additions to scriptural law, contrasting these traditions with what the Bible commands. But already the disparagement of purity washings in Mark's explanation at the beginning comes close to disparaging ritual washing altogether, including those enjoined in Scripture. This suspicion is confirmed in what follows next. Here Mark returns to what was probably Jesus' original response to the complaint: not what enters but what comes out of a person makes a person unclean (7:14-15). With Jesus it was doubtless a matter of degree, as we have seen. He was not advocating neglect of the food laws enshrined in Scripture, but making the point that they were not nearly as important as impurity within a person. But by Mark's time the contrast had become sharper and more absolute. Jesus' words were now being understood as declaring that food cannot make a person unclean. We see this in the way that the saying has been explained in 7:17-22. There the point is made that food is just food; its enters the stomach and goes out into the toilet. There is a strong element of ridicule here. The impurity that matters is in people's attitude and behavior. Just in case people miss the point, Mark adds that in saying all of this Jesus is "declaring all foods clean" (7:19c).

Dispensing with Scripture That Discriminates

The effect of the whole is to reject large parts of the biblical law as irrelevant and invalid, especially those concerned with ritual purity and with foods. The argument is not that these were temporary, but that they never were valid because such external things can never make a person unclean. It is an attack on the fundamental notion that such categories count. By dismissing such distinctions a major obstacle is removed that had prevented the inclusion of Gentiles in the people of God. Mark does not go so far as Paul and say that we are no longer under the Law, but he comes close to it and in his own distinctive way. For Mark it is less a question of no longer being under the Law and more the fact that such laws never made sense. Nothing like that counts. What alone counts is ethical purity in the context of love for God and one's neighbor.

Mark — Betraying the Bible?

This teaching removes the barriers that separated Jew and Gentile. That was Mark's view and Paul's before him. We should not be under the illusion that all other Christians or Jews, for that matter, would have agreed. Many, including many Christians of the time, would find what Mark has done outrageous. The Scripture did not have to be hacked about to enable Gentiles to be included. There were lots of Gentiles who attended synagogues and a good number of them converted fully to Judaism, following the path, if they were male, of being circumcised and taking on themselves the yoke of the Law as God's gift of guidance for the holy life. It was not true that Gentiles were excluded. There were ways for them to become part of the people of God, and they could then live on the same basis as every other Jew in obedience to God's word. There was no need to tamper with Scripture. To suggest that God had given laws that were inadequate or temporary, or worse still, nonsensical, was outrageous if not blasphemous.

Mark laid himself open to the charge of betraying his own people (if he was a Jew) or, at least, betraying Scripture. It would not be hard to point the finger at his reasons for making such changes. He was too much influenced by the rationalist tendencies of the intellectual world of the day, which ridiculed religious rites, and he watered down what the Bible said to make it easier to increase his church membership. Shame!

In Defense of Mark

For Mark, it does not seem that he is in the heat of the debate. It seems long since settled. He is only reflecting what had come to be widely accepted in his circles and portraying Jesus' attitudes accordingly. The days of Paul were when the debate was at its peak, two decades earlier. Some of the materials passed down to him already reflected the new freedom and attributed it to Jesus. What are we to say? What they attributed to Jesus was false? At one level one would have to agree. As we have seen, Jesus' concerns were about priorities; he did not advocate rejection of any part of Scripture.

Yet, in Mark's defense, one could argue that by putting compassion at the heart of spirituality Jesus introduced or reaffirmed something that would inevitably lead to the kind of thing Paul and Mark espoused. The starting point in dealing with non-Jews was discriminatory, and telling people they must first become Jews to be acceptable reinforced this discrimination, even if that was what Scripture demanded. Already during his ministry Jesus had given higher priority to human need in some instances than to keeping purity laws. In his situation that did not amount to rejection of those laws. It is quite common to be faced with a decision between two competing laws. Wherever this happened, Jesus chose to put direct compassion first, even if at times after a struggle. With the new situation the church found itself in, the issue became more than a few exceptional instances. People were having to decide what would be the norm. It was as a result of this kind of pressure that most early Christians agreed at least to drop the requirement of circumcision.

Mark in Line with Paul

But food was an important part of daily life and played a central role in Christian communities. Paul pushed on and declared that the ad hoc practice of Christian Jews and Gentiles dining together should be maintained; in Antioch, when people from James in Jerusalem raised the issue, Peter and most others reverted to being separate. We now read about it in Galatians 2:11-14. We have no way of knowing whether the writer we call Mark knew of this episode. But we can be sure he would have sided with Paul in the debate. Neither Paul nor Mark saw their stance as a contradiction of what Jesus stood for. On the contrary they saw it as an extension of what Jesus set at the heart of his gospel: God's compassion for all without discrimination. Paul argued directly that the gospel of Jesus did not demand Gentiles to become Jews, but treated all on the same level.

Why Mark Took Such an Approach to Scripture

Behind Mark's stance are two further factors, which also play a role for Paul. They are, to begin with, the authority attributed to Jesus. Jesus had so moved into the center of Mark's thought that he felt free to reject parts of Scripture he saw as inconsistent with Jesus' approach. He not only espoused Jesus' approach to Scripture, but took it further. Before him Paul had acted in a similar way. Jesus rather than Scripture had become the main source of authority; it was not so much that a body of Jesus' sayings replaced Scripture, but that Jesus' attitude became the primary point of reference. This is especially clear in Paul, who knows only a few sayings of Jesus.

The second aspect is what I cited above as a likely accusation by Mark's opponents: Mark was too influenced by the rationalist climate of the day, which rejected the relevance of external rites and ceremonies. In Mark's defense one could argue that this kind of thing was already present in Jesus' teaching. It explains why he gave a higher priority to commands concerned with care for people than those concerned with maintaining ritual purity. In this he was in good company with many of his day and with much of Scripture, which put special emphasis on justice and compassion. Already within Israel there was considerable sensitivity on the issue. Pagan religions were rejected for their immorality. Their idols and cultic practices were spurned. There were frequent challenges against tendencies within Israel to forget that God cannot be held in temples made by human hands (1 Kings 8:27; Isa. 66:1). Sacrifices without commitment to justice are an abomination (Amos 5:21-24; Hos. 6:6; Ps. 40:6-8). Circumcision of the heart mattered far more than circumcision of the flesh (Deut. 10:16; Jer. 4:4). A contrite heart mattered more than many sacrifices (Ps. 51:16-17).

Mark in Line with Jesus?

Jesus stood in this tradition. It had not yet developed to the point where the contrast had become absolute. It was almost without exception a matter of keeping the whole, but putting the priority on relationship with God expressed in right ethical behavior. In Jesus' day (and perhaps earlier as well) such awareness was also kept alive by the impact of other cultures. In the Hellenistic Roman world it was impossible to escape foreign influences. They reached into every part of life. Non-English speakers today can identify the feeling immediately:

borrowed words, fashions, educational trends, and so on; English-speaking American culture is all pervasive. Even in conservative Jewish Palestine the Hellenistic practice of reclining for meals had long since established itself. The Jewish city rebuilt by Herod Antipas at Sepphoris a few kilometers from Jesus' hometown was designed and constructed on Hellenistic models. Scattered around the Galilee region were Gentile cities, especially the Decapolis (the ten cities) to the east, replete with pagan temples and pagan practices. Lower Galilee was on a major trade route. Travel was not uncommon. A Gentile centurion was at home in Capernaum. In addition, Jews were settled in almost every part of the empire and beyond. While generally maintaining a strong sense of identity, not least through practices that set them apart, most Jews could not help but have some encounter with other religions.

Responding to Different Cultures

Responses to such cross-cultural encounter varied from defensive withdrawal, as in the community that withdrew to the shores of the Dead Sea, to downright assimilation to the dominant culture. A common phenomenon in religion in such situations is that a distinction emerges between what is peculiar to one's own culture and what is universally applicable. People then either emphasize what is particularly theirs or what is universally applicable. Where the latter occurs, you find an emphasis on ethics, whereas in the former the emphasis falls on specific rites and special places. Within this spectrum Jesus appears to belong more strongly with those who emphasize the universal. Such cross-cultural experience doubtless played a role in the universal and ethical focus of wisdom and prophetic streams of thought in ancient Israel.

It is interesting that when a religion becomes culturally mobile, as did Christianity, it has to grapple with what to retain and what to discard. It then needs to become enculturated in its new cultural setting. From there the whole process repeats itself or, at least, the issues are raised afresh. In many respects Christianity succeeded in enculturating itself into the West; its problem, among other things, is that in many respects it has become culturally immobile. Cultural mobility is not just a matter of passing from one nation to another. It is frequently a matter within a nation.

Cultural mobility is an acute issue within nations like Australia and America. In grappling with such issues we find ourselves frequently concerned with identity markers and cultural particularities. In many respects divisions among the churches over orders of ministry, liturgy and celebration, forms of government, reflect the passions of those who would have also experienced Jesus and Mark as a threat. The cultural particularities, including the revival of absolutes about holy space, holy personnel, holy order, have taken Christianity, in my view, back beyond its origins to a point where it has most in common with those in Judaism and in the early church who resisted the likes of Jesus, Paul, and Mark.

Both Paul and Mark are among the universalizers who have contributed to the cultural mobility of Christianity. Paul pleads for the markers to be dropped. He directly alludes to the biblical image of circumcision of the heart, but unlike Deuteronomy and Jeremiah, he applies it exclusively to dropping the requirement of circumcision. In Mark 7 the relativizing of externals has become a disparagement of externals. Such things in themselves have no inherent worth.

A Spiritual Temple Replaces the Physical Temple

The other major area where we see Mark's approach come to the fore is in his treatment of the temple. In Mark's account of Jesus' trial before the high priest false witnesses report that Jesus had said: "I will destroy this temple made with hands and in three days build another temple not made with hands" (14:58). As we discussed in the previous chapter, the falsity of the statement is the claim that Jesus himself would destroy the temple.

It was not false that Jesus predicted the temple's destruction (he did so in Mark 13) nor, according to Mark, that he made the contrast between a temple made with hands with one not made with hands. In speaking of the latter, Mark's value system reemerges. A temple made by human hands is just that and nothing more. Mark is quite happy to have Jesus speak of it as God's house and to describe its intended function as a house of prayer for all peoples (11:17). Already in this allusion to Isaiah we see Mark's priorities of inclusiveness. Mark is happy to see the temple function as a place of prayer for all peoples, but not with what has happened to it. It has become a den of robbers. It is tempting to use the word "brigands" instead of robbers, because the Greek word that Mark used certainly also carried that connotation. Mark probably knew that during the revolt against Rome, A.D. 66-70, very close to Mark's time of writing, revolutionary groups had taken over the temple. Perhaps Mark intends such a "wink," just as he alerts the reader to these events in Mark 13.

But in the context of the story of Jesus, the words are addressed to Jesus' contemporaries and must make sense there. There they attack what the temple had become. From the rest of Mark we see that the temple houses a system that exploits the poor in favor of the rich and so stands under God's judgment. From Mark's perspective there are two things wrong here: corruption and the very notion that the temple is more than a human construction for the purpose of prayer. Its system of sacrifices and purity laws, though based on Scripture, has no validity. This emerges clearly when we consider the way Mark has composed 11:1–13:38.

The Spiritual Temple: The Christian Community

Jesus enters Jerusalem and goes immediately to the temple to look around (11:11). The temple was, after all, the center of Israel's religion. Jesus saw it as God's house. When Jesus departs, a new episode begins. Like the episode we discussed earlier about Jesus' family and about the accusation that Jesus was in league with demons, this episode has two parts. The account of Jesus' action in the temple (11:15-18) is sandwiched between the account of Jesus' cursing a fig tree (11:12-14) and its resultant shriveling (11:19-25). The result is that the cursing of the fig tree functions as a symbolic commentary on what happens in the temple.

Jesus hopes to find fruit on the tree, but finds none; it is cursed (11:12-14). Symbolically Mark is indicating that God's judgment will fall on the temple because it fails to bear fruit. It fails to be what it should be. Next follows the event in which Jesus overturns the money-changers' tables, drives away those selling pigeons, and stops the busy traffic in the temple courtyard (11:15-18). His words indicate that he thinks the temple has ceased to function in the way it should. In Mark the attack is not primarily on individual dealers and traders but on the system they represent, which has become exploitative. The next day the disciples find the tree shriveled (11:20). The point is obvious. It is then no surprise that Jesus goes on to a discussion about prayer and forgiveness (11:21-25). For in Mark's view the new community of believers will become a spiritual temple, one not made with human hands. It will become a house of prayer for all people, fulfilling the temple's original purpose.

A Temple Built on the Foundation of Jesus

The same theme keeps reemerging in the encounters that follow. First comes a challenge to Jesus' authority for doing what he did in the temple (11:27-33). Jesus responds by linking his own authority to that of John. Both had, of course, posed problems for the temple authorities because they offered grace outside the normal channels. Jesus continues his answer in 12:1-12 in a daring parable about the keepers of a vineyard who failed to make its produce available to the owner. The imagery is subtle. Isaiah had used the image of the vineyard to represent Israel (Isa. 5:1-2). Jesus, in Mark, uses it in order not to attack Israel, but its keepers — the temple authorities. Their role is to be replaced by a new people who will make sure the produce is available. The parable also includes the gruesome murder of the owner's beloved son, a scarcely veiled allusion to the impending execution of Jesus. Appended to the parable is the image drawn from Psalm 118:22. The stone the builders rejected has become the foundation stone. One can scarcely miss the allusion to the new temple that will replace the old.

The Messiah and the New Temple

The next episode, which relates to the temple directly, comes in 12:28-34. Here a sympathetic scribe reaches consensus with Jesus that the chief commandments are love for God and love for neighbor. When the scribe states that these matter more than burnt offerings and sacrifices, he was alluding to a stance well founded in Scripture (e.g., Hos. 6:6). Mark, however, would have understood these words more radically. For him sacrifices and burnt offerings did not matter at all. In this sense he would understand Jesus' words, that the scribe was not far from the kingdom of God, as indicating that there was still some considerable distance to go.

This episode and the next, where Jesus speaks of messiahship (12:35-37), foreshadow the issue that will come up at Jesus' trial: the temple and messiahship. The link between the two may be traditional. One role attributed to the messiah was that he would build or rebuild the temple. The link goes back to Nathan's prophecy to David in 2 Samuel 7, that his son would reign after him and would build the temple. People had come to see in 2 Samuel 7 also a prediction of the future Son of David, who as messiah would sit on David's throne and, like Solomon, act to restore or build the temple. According to Mark, the new temple this messiah would build would be the community of the church.

Announcing the Temple's Destruction

The temple remains in focus in 12:38-44, where Mark first reports Jesus' attack on the temple leaders for their exploitation of the poor and widows and then contrasts this with a humble widow devoutly offering all she has to the temple. The contrast screams out! It makes a powerful transition to Mark 13, in which Mark reports Jesus' prediction that the temple will face destruction. It is a deft touch that Mark introduces the chapter by describing how the disciples are now looking around in the temple, just as Jesus had in 11:11. Mark alerts the reader to the fact that the events of his own time are bringing this dire prediction to fulfillment.

We have already noticed how the temple theme reappears at Jesus' Jewish trial. It appears for the last time during Mark's account of the crucifixion. Those who mock Jesus recall the accusation at his trial: "Ha, you who would destroy the temple and rebuild it in three days, save yourself and come down from the cross!" (15:30). The answer comes a few lines later. At Jesus' death the curtain is torn from top to bottom (15:38). Judgment is prefigured.

Discarding the Temple System
Discards Parts of Biblical Law

Mark's treatment of the temple is twofold. He picks up and expands Jesus' attack on its corruption. But, in addition, he applies to it the value system implicit in Mark 7. Thus he sees its value only as a place of prayer. The corruption and abuse have prevented it from being even this. Its sacrifices and systems of purity are irrelevant here, as are such things as washing hands before meals. It makes no difference that they are biblically based.

Disparaging All Externals?

In the context of the recent history, in which his Christianity had torn itself from its Jewish roots and resolved to affirm Scripture only selectively and set the attitude of Christ as its ultimate authority, Mark can hardly be expected to offer a balanced reappraisal of Jewish religious culture. It is clear that Mark does not disparage all symbolic actions. He speaks affirmingly of John's baptism and probably knew the practice of Christian baptism. His account of the Last Supper probably reflects the practice of Holy Communion in his community (14:22-25). He does not speak disparagingly of the Passover. The temple had a legitimate place. So it is wrong to say that Mark disparaged externals as such. On the other hand, he does disparage some practices. Making distinctions among foods, among ritual washing of hands and implements, belong to practices to which Mark gives no special place. In Mark's system of thinking such practices have no inherent spiritual worth and may be discarded. The same would apply to much that went on in the temple. We should also be cautious about assuming that Mark had faced all the issues and worked them all through to a point of complete consistency.

Discriminating Within Scripture
in the Light of Core Values

With regard to his attitude towards the law, and the Scripture in particular, the following features emerge. Mark is prepared to discard significant chunks of Scripture, but clearly holds on to others. It cannot have been a popular stance, but it was one that put him in Paul's company; as we have seen, both drew their inspiration from the attitude of Jesus. If we ask about the criteria that governed their approach, we find that it was really a combination. There was the centrality of compassion — the attitude of Jesus — which they were prepared to take further than Jesus because they faced new situations not on his horizon. In addition, there was a value system that gave greater priority to ethical law in contrast to ritual law. Here, too, Mark went beyond Jesus in moving from an inclusive to an exclusive contrast. Playing a role in this step for Mark was a stronger sense that purity laws concerned themselves with matters that had no real bearing on spirituality and could be ignored. The awareness that these were peculiarities of their own culture may well have contributed to the attitude of both Jesus and Mark. But for

Mark, that culture could be left behind without loss, whereas it was still part of Jesus.

Thus Mark offers a challenging model for interpreting Scripture. It entails putting Christ at the center and understanding him as implying that what matters most to God is people. It also entails a willingness to apply this critically to Scripture itself — not only to set priorities among scriptural commands, as Jesus did, but also, where necessary, to abandon scriptural commands, especially those that can no longer seem valid either because of their substance or because they stand in conflict with the inclusive tendency of the gospel of Jesus. Mark celebrates the inclusion of Gentiles in his community made possible in Mark's view by the discarding of the complex system of purity laws. It is probably right to assume that Mark's community would also have included women fully and many others.

Risking Mark's Alternative to Fundamentalism

The Markan approach to biblical interpretation is reflected in Christians' later handling of parts of the New Testament that preserve discriminatory attitudes and practices. The issues have included slavery, the place of women in the church, and more recently — amid much ongoing debate — homosexuality. But the approach regularly comes under fire, and its advocates must continually struggle with the danger of discarding too much.

Mark is perhaps on safer ground than Paul in this respect, but many would ask whether it is too great a risk to interpret the Scripture on the basis of an alleged attitude of Jesus and of God. I think it is a risk worth taking and necessary, but one can understand when others have sought to build in greater safeguards. As we shall see, Matthew and Luke are good examples of this. Away from the heat of the first century we might want to speak less disparagingly of other people's cultures than does Mark. That would include reappraisal of the value of various cultural practices and the way they function for people.

Mark would be disappointed, I am sure, if we failed to recognize

that much of what Christianity has become consists of such particularities. But even here we can learn from Mark without becoming icono-
clastic. In my view our cultural traditions come into their own when
we value them for what they are and let them be, without pressing
them into absolutes. Ultimately this is also the age-old problem at the
heart of handling the Scripture itself. But then I speak, here, under the
shadow of Mark.

• 3 •

Q

Dispensing with Nothing, but Getting the Priorities Right

One of the most valuable sources of the gospels is known to us simply as Q. "Q" is the first letter of the German word "Quelle," which means "Source." It reflects the fact that much of the initial research done in this area in the early nineteenth century was done in the German language. I share the view of most New Testament scholars that there was indeed such a document, and that it was used as a major source by Matthew and Luke when they wrote their gospels. Even though we do not possess manuscripts of Q, it has been possible to reach broad agreement on what it contained. For the purpose of my discussion I shall assume the reconstruction recently formulated by the Society of Biblical Literature International Q Project (see Robinson under *Further Reading*).

It is generally agreed that Luke has stayed more closely with Q's original order, as he does also with Mark. Matthew often appears to have subjected the wording of Q to less revision. It is not possible in the scope of this study to pursue the kind of detailed analysis that lies behind such reconstruction. It is sufficient to assume Q's existence in something like the order and arrangement and form of words recently reconstructed by the Q Project.

My purpose will be not only to look at Q's stance but also at what it might tell us about the stance of Jesus himself, and to include in that discussion related material from other traditions which the gospels include, just as we did in discussing the material behind Mark.

John the Baptist

Q begins with the striking report of John the Baptist. Unlike Mark's account, which speaks in summary of John's call to repentance, Q preserves some of John's statements. "You generation of vipers, who warned you to flee from the coming wrath? So produce fruit worthy of repentance; and don't say among yourselves, 'We have Abraham as our father'; for I tell you, God can raise up children to Abraham from these stones!" (Q 3:7-8; cf. Matt. 3:7-9; Luke 3:7-8). No one is privileged. Don't get a false sense of security based on being Abraham's people. Nothing can substitute for proper repentance. John's call is thoroughly biblical and stands in line with the prophets who similarly challenged a false sense of security. John is not attacking Abraham or people's sense of belonging to the family of Abraham. He is simply saying that it counts for nothing if people do not obey God's will. Obeying God's will means keeping God's will as set out in Scripture. Nothing suggests that John had some other teaching in mind.

The way Q proceeds makes it clear that John had the biblical commandments in mind. For after what must have been a brief mention of Jesus' baptism, but which has not been preserved, Q reports the temptations of Jesus in the wilderness where the same theme emerges. Jesus is totally obedient to God's will and in response to each temptation cites a passage from Deuteronomy. Q's account of John's teaching reinforces the demand for repentance accompanied by obedience. "Already the axe lies at the root of the tree; every tree which does not produce good fruit shall be cut down and thrown into the fire" (Q 3:9; cf. Matt. 3:10; Luke 3:9). John goes on to announce the coming of the executioner who will gather the wheat, burn up the chaff, and subject people to a baptism of fire and the Holy Spirit (Q 3:16-17; cf. Matt. 3:11-12; Luke 3:16-17).

John and Jesus

Q allies John and Jesus, both by this prediction and by the event that immediately follows. Jesus is the coming executioner of whom John spoke. By baptizing Jesus John confirms this identity. This has the effect of also making Jesus a strong advocate of the demands of God's Law, and as we have already noted, the temptation story further reinforces this identification. Jesus refuses to use divine power to meet his own needs to relieve his fast. He refuses to test out God's power by pulling a stunt in the temple. He refuses all other authority except God's. Jesus identifies himself firmly as God's Son who is intent on doing God's will, obeying God's will as set forth in Scripture. As already mentioned, all of Jesus' responses derive from Deuteronomy and emphasize the stance of total obedience to God's word as the source of life. This fits the emphasis given by John to keeping God's commands.

John's Problem

There is an immediate problem: John announces Jesus as the executioner; but Jesus does not play the role of an executioner. There is no winnowing fan in his hand. He wields no ax. There is no baptism of destruction. In Q, Jesus' next action after the temptations is to teach his disciples, not to bring judgment. He then heals the centurion at Capernaum. It is little wonder that Q next reports that John sent some of his disciples to ask Jesus if he really was the one he had predicted. Jesus' response is an important statement: "Go and tell John what you hear and see: the blind receive their sight again and the lame walk, lepers are made clean and the deaf hear, and the dead are raised and poor people are told good news; and blessed is the one who takes no offence at me" (Q 7:22-23; Matt. 11:4-6; Luke 7:22-23).

This reply is a patchwork of allusions to Old Testament prophecies about hope (Isa. 26:19; 29:18-19; 35:5-6; 42:6-7; 61:1). The effect is to tell John that such hope is being fulfilled and that John should not take offense that things are not quite working out the way John had envisaged them. Up to this point Q had mentioned only a few of these things: Jesus proclaimed good news to the poor when he declared, "Blessed are you poor, for yours is the kingdom of God" (Luke 6:20; cf. Matt. 5:3; Luke 6:20). And in healing the centurion's servant (Q 7:1-10; cf. Matt. 8:5-13; Luke 7:1-10) he had virtually raised him from the dead. But the community that used Q must have known of other healings.

The striking thing is that Jesus does not meet John's expectations, yet claims to be the one that John predicted. What we see here is a change of emphasis. It is not a split between John and Jesus. You can see that by what immediately follows, where Jesus talks about John and hails him as a prophet and more than a prophet, as the greatest human being ever born (Q 11:28; cf. Matt. 11:11; Luke 11:28). Even the distinction that follows in the same verse, which argues that the least person in the kingdom of God is greater than John, should not be seen as an undermining of John's authority. The difference is between one era and the next. John, like the prophets of old, belongs to an era that looks forward to the days of fulfillment; in Jesus those days of fulfillment have begun to be reality.

Responses to John and Jesus

Q underlines the close link between Jesus and John in the parable of the children in the marketplace who were angry with their fellows for not dancing to their tune (Q 7:31-35; cf. Matt. 11:16-19; Luke 7:31-35). Both John and Jesus are the butt of criticism; they both belong together; they reflect God's wisdom. But it is also notable that their behavior is in sharp contrast. This contrast matches the contrast between John's predictions and expectations and Jesus' actual performance. People attack John for his severe asceticism, for living sparely; people attack Jesus for indulging freely in food and drink. The contrast is an important clue about the attitude of each. John's behavior fitted someone waiting for something to come. Prayer and fasting were common features of such a stance. Jesus' behavior fitted someone who is celebrating the arrival of what had been hoped for. In discussing Mark we noticed that the same issue arose when John's disciples questioned why Jesus did not fast and Jesus responded by saying: you don't fast at a wedding banquet (Mark 2:19).

Q and the Bible

What does this tell us about the attitude towards the Bible in Q? Clearly John and Jesus agree in demanding total obedience to God's will. But how that works itself depends on the perspective of each. John's focus is on judgment and warning. Jesus' emphasis is on hope, on activities that make people whole, on celebration and joy. But it would be quite wrong to deny that Jesus speaks of judgment. Q envisages that one day God's judgment will come; but in Jesus' preaching and ministry hope and healing predominate. It is a matter of emphasis. Q is in no doubt that both demand the fulfillment of God's will and command as set forth in Scripture.

This becomes particularly clear in a passage that brings together John, the Law and the Prophets, the Kingdom of God: "The law and [[ ]] the prophets . . . until John. From [[then]] the kingdom of God has suffered violence and the violent take it by force. But it is easier for heaven and earth to pass away than for [[ ]] one stroke of the law to <<lose its force>>" (Q 16:16-17; cf. Matt. 11:12-13; 5:18; Luke 16:16-17). The new thing is the kingdom of God, which comes with Jesus. It does not replace the Law and the Prophets and their demands; nor does it annul John and his. On the contrary, the coming of God's reign has heightened the battle. This is why Jesus adds that not a single stroke of the Law is to fall. Its demands stand firm.

In Q Jesus immediately gives an instance: divorce. "Everyone who divorces his wife [[ ]] commit[[s]] adultery, and the one who marries a divorcée [[ ]] commits adultery" (Q 16:18; cf. Luke 16:18; Matt. 5:32). In other words, the Law is to be upheld strictly; in fact, in this case, it is to be upheld even more strictly than the letter of the Law demands. Q goes on to report Jesus' comments about people who commit offenses and how they might be forgiven. Not only what follows, but also what precedes these words of Jesus about the Law shows the overriding concern about obedience: "No one can serve two masters; for either he will hate the one and love the other or hold fast to the one and despise the other. You cannot serve God and mammon" (Q 16:13; cf. Matt. 6:24). This coheres well with the attack on divorce, which represented an abuse of women — often for monetary gain.

Jesus and the Pharisees

The strict line on upholding scriptural commands comes through very strongly in Jesus' encounter with the Pharisees. He begins in Q on the subject of tithing: "But woe to you Pharisees, for you tithe mint and [[dill]] and [[cumin]] and neglect justice and the love of God; these you ought to have done while not neglecting those" (Q 11:42; cf. Matt. 23:23; Luke 11:42). These Pharisees are seeking to apply biblical tithing laws to every area of life, even to herbs. Jesus attacks this preoccupation with such detail because they are neglecting what he considers paramount. In other words, in obeying Scripture commands it is more important to ask what justice and love of God mean in everyday life than to ask how tithing laws apply. But we should not misconstrue Jesus' answer. He does not oppose such tithing. He even says, "while not neglecting those." Q and its community clearly assumed that Scripture commands about tithing were to be applied to everyday life. The question was one of priority.

It is worth reflecting that some might have said: "There can be no such priority that weighs some commands of God above others. All should be treated as equally authoritative, since all are God given. What is more, you raise the issue of love for God; it is precisely by obeying God's commands to the finest detail that we demonstrate that we love God." This is not Q's view. Q portrays Jesus as definitively setting priorities, but not excluding let alone disparaging any commands.

Jesus offers a similar challenge to the Pharisees to change their emphasis when he speaks of purification: "Woe to you Pharisees, for you cleanse the outside of the cup and the dish, but the inside is full from grasping and lack of self control. . . . Did not he who made the outside also make the inside?" (Q 11:39-40; cf. Matt. 23:25-26; Luke 11:39-40). The attack is on the hypocrisy of giving attention to ritual cleansing while ignoring ethical purity. Again, it is not a matter of either or, but of both and; both ritual and ethical purity are required. The attacks on abuses continue. People who adorn the tombs of prophets ought to heed what they teach. We even read that Jesus acknowledged that the Pharisees had "the keys," probably, "of knowledge"; this was probably a reference to the Bible as they had it (Q 11:52; cf. Matt. 23:13; Luke 11:52). The problem was that they failed to apply it rightly. In their hands people were made to carry difficult burdens, probably legal rulings based on Scripture, but received no care in the process: "Woe to you [[<Pharisees>]], for [[you load]] people with burdens hard to bear, and you yourselves with [[ ]] your finger [[ ]] do not <move> them" (Q 11:46; cf. Matt. 23:4; Luke 11:46).

Conflict and Danger

The conflict with the Pharisees is particularly sharp. They emerge both as religious leaders, whose status and responsibility is not questioned, and as the kind of people who killed prophets and — one can hardly miss the allusion — will help to contribute to the death of Jesus: "Therefore also the wisdom . . . said, 'I shall send . . . them prophets and apostles, and some of them they will kill and persecute, so that the blood of all the prophets poured out from the foundation of the world will be required of this generation'" (Q 11:49-51; cf. Matt. 23:34-36; Luke 11:49-51; cf. also Q 13:34-35; cf. Matt. 23:37-39; Luke 13:34-35). It is an extraordinary warning and may reflect the author's view of events that have befallen the Jewish state in his time. But it is not the statement of an outsider. It is made as a statement of Jesus, an insider, who upholds the whole Law and insists that the problem is in no way the Law or the commandments, but their abuse and the failure to give priority to what mattered most.

A Matter of Priorities

We are back with the issue of priorities. The Jesus we meet in Q demands that the biblical law be kept in its entirety, but within a certain perspective which reflected a scale of priorities. We meet these priorities elsewhere in Q. There is some uncertainty whether Q contained an anecdote about the sabbath. The following may originally belong in a controversy about healing on the sabbath: "Which of you who has a cow, if it fell into a deep hole on the sabbath would not rescue it?" (Q 14:5; cf. Matt. 12:11-12; Luke 14:5). The argument here is the appropriate application of sabbath law.

In Q, the priorities in Jesus' approach are not to be found mainly in controversies, but rather in instructions to his disciples. They come to us now in the form of instructions for disciples, because that will have been their function within the early Christian communities that used the material. At their core they are teachings of Jesus, and they probably had a wider audience in mind. The first major collection of such teachings comes in Q immediately after Jesus' temptations (Q 6:20-23, 27-49; cf. Matt. 5–7; Luke 6:20-49). They are the first report of Jesus' teaching and therefore all the more important. In Q they come at a point where the hearer has been introduced to Jesus through John as one who, with John, champions God's will and who has faithfully done God's will in the face of temptation. This gives the block of teaching that follows the character of instruction coming from the one designated by John as he who will exercise divine judgment. But we also need to consider this group of sayings in its own right, especially as we consider what might have been its significance on the lips of the historical Jesus.

Hope

The group of sayings begins with promise, not the warning tone we might have expected after John's introduction. Jesus declares: "Blessed are you poor, for yours is the kingdom of God; blessed are you who hunger, for you shall be satisfied; blessed are you who weep, now for you shall laugh" (Q 6:20-21; cf. Matt. 5:3-12; Luke 3:20-21). As in John, the focus is still on the future; but the focus is hope not warning. We meet again the central theme of God's reign, which was so prominent in Mark's traditions. The substance of this hope is quite down to earth. It will be good for poor and hungry people. Things will change for them. Weeping will turn to joy. When God reigns, there will be a transformation of present realities. So much is being said here about God and therefore about God's priorities and Jesus' priorities. God's will is about such a transformation. This sheds light on the meaning of Jesus' challenge to the Pharisees about the way they approach Scripture: what matters most is not minute tithing but "justice and the love of God" (Q 11:42; cf. Matt. 23:23; Luke 11:42).

A fourth blessing is pronounced on the disciples who will face persecution for their faith (Q 6:22-23; cf. Matt. 5:11-12; Luke 6:22-23). Here we see the process of what were promises addressed to the crowd being applied later to the Christian communities. The focus shifts to reward in heaven. A similar twofold focus is evident in the teaching about enemies that immediately follows. It is now couched as advice to persecuted Christians and how they should respond. But underlying it is Jesus' approach to people. Enemies are not to be hated. Retaliation should be avoided. We should treat people the way we want them to treat us. Loving only one's own is to do no better than the toll collectors and the Gentiles. Here we see another trace of the conservatism of the historical Jesus, who assumes a low view of the morality of such groups. To this point we have before us practical advice, but then follows a reason: we should try to be like God, who makes no discrimination among people when it comes to rain and sunshine (Q 6:35; cf. Matt. 5:45). We should be compassionate as God is compassionate. The collection ends with warnings about judging others and about the consequences of neglecting Jesus' teaching. Much of this in Q applies to the ongoing Christian communities and their leadership.

This collection of sayings forms the nucleus for Matthew's Sermon on the Mount. Compared with Matthew's version, the Q collection makes next to no reference to Scripture. It is a combination of sayings that reflect practical wisdom (the golden rule) and a theology that emphasizes God's compassion. Even with the latter, the grounds for such theology are not the great epic accounts of God's action in history, but daily events of nature. The promises to the destitute come closer to reflecting biblical passages — the prophets in particular, but the statements are made to stand on their own, not as expositions of the written word.

Jesus' Teaching and Scripture Teaching

As we turn to other parts of Q, we find a number of similar instances where the teaching of Jesus seems to stand on its own. In his instruction about prayer Jesus likens God to a father who, like any good father, will surely respond to the needs of a child (Q 11:11-13; cf. Matt. 7:9-11; Luke 11:11-13). Jesus offers comfort to the anxious by reminding them of God's care for sparrows and even for the hairs of a person's head (Q 12:6-7; cf. Matt. 10:29-31; Luke 12:6-7). The birds and the flowers teach trust in God's goodness (Q 12:22-31; cf. Matt. 6:25-33; Luke 12:22-31). God is like a shepherd who will care about the lost sheep (Q 15:4; cf. Matt. 18:12-13; Luke 15:3-7).

What we are encountering in this material is a major characteristic of Jesus' teaching: the use of everyday experience as a basis for theological reflection. In particular, Jesus draws images from daily life in order to expound his message. Sometimes it is a single image, as in the comparison with a caring father; sometimes it becomes a story. To stay with the image of the father, this is best known in Jesus' parable of the prodigal son (Luke 15:11-32). People would have been familiar with young men wanting to go abroad. In the Roman empire of the time there were settlements of Jews in most centers of population. So it was quite feasible to journey to a foreign land. The anguish and grief of parents would have found a ready echo, even if, as with many of Jesus' parables, some details of how it came about were exaggerated for the story. The story worked because it was both realistic and shocking. It was shocking that the father dropped the usual dignity of male demeanor and ran to embrace his son. But it was also the most natural thing in the world. Jesus was appealing to a theology based on the best imaginable in human relations as a base point. The objections of the elder brother are also realistic and help sharpen the issue between two different attitudes towards what is right. What is justice?

Another of Jesus' parables presses this point even further and again begins with the familiar: unemployment (Matt. 20:1-16). Workers hired for various lengths of time over a single day all receive a full day's wage. What matters most: equity of reward or what one needs to live? Jesus is famous for such stories. The parable of the Good Samaritan (Luke 10:30-37) is a further example of a familiar scenario laced with surprises. The main surprise is the Samaritan hero who shows friendship. Another is the negative treatment accorded the religious personnel, with the implication that their religious concerns lead them to miss the point of what, for Jesus, religion is all about. These stories worked because they appealed to commonly held values. It was not that people had never thought about practical acts of compassion before. They had. Many of Jesus' themes about God's goodness, about trust, about showing friendship, find their echoes in popular teaching of the time, among both Jews and non-Jews.

Jesus as Popular Teacher of His Day

This extends so far that some scholars have suggested that perhaps Jesus drew his main inspiration from non-Jews and that he should be seen primarily as a very creative exponent of such values. They point to a string of similarities between the way Jesus confronted religious authorities of his day and the practice of many similarly itinerant preachers and teachers of the Hellenistic world who poked fun at the hypocrisy and pretension of the powerful. They, too, are reported to have been dinner guests of the rich and sometimes the scandalous. They, too, trod the streets in very basic attire, not unlike the limited attire enjoined of the disciples. Jesus may well have stood under such influence, however that may have come about. Unfortunately, how this may have happened remains a matter of speculation. Galilee was certainly open to Hellenistic influence. It is hard, however, to imagine the conservative Jewish Jesus keeping company with popular pagan teachers. The point of connection for a conservative Jew might have been a shared disdain of idolatrous religious systems and everything associated with them.

But Judaism also had its strong tradition of common wisdom; for centuries it had been an area where much foreign influence penetrated Israelite thought, beginning with the collections of sayings in Proverbs. The wisdom of Sirach shares in this heritage, but with a very strong emphasis on the need to keep God's Law. In the sayings of Jesus such exhortations to heed the written Law are rare. Yet without doubt Jesus would have seen his teaching, including his common sense teaching about ethics and about God and trust, as thoroughly consistent with Israel's heritage, and in the broadest sense as expounding God's Law. Much of the imagery he uses has its roots in the Old Testament: harvest, shepherd, vineyard. There are also allusions in his wisdom sayings to biblical figures such as Solomon (who else?). Nothing suggests that Jesus saw his teaching as doing anything other than expounding God's will.

This means that Jesus approached his own religious culture in a very interesting way. It is even more appropriate to speak of his expounding the heritage of Israel than to speak of his approach to Scripture. Jesus was not a scribe who expounded particular pieces of Scripture. He taught more generally, drawing widely on popular insight and experience. But he did so on a consistent base that was formed by two major concerns. First was the message of kingdom. The second was the way he thought about God.

The Message of the Kingdom

While "kingdom of God" has become the standard expression, it is better to say God's reign, because then we can avoid putting an idea or a place at the center of his thought. Rather, God is at the center of his thought, and in particular God's action in the future. Thus Jesus encourages his disciples to pray: "Your kingdom come!" (Matt. 6:10; Luke 11:2). In sending out the disciples he instructs them that they are to announce, "The kingdom of God is at hand" (Matt. 10:7; Luke 10:9, 11). Jesus saw his healing activity as signs that already God's rule was asserting itself. He speaks of his exorcisms as moments when the reign of God had become reality (Matt. 12:28; Luke 11:20). Since John the Baptist the reign of God had been embroiled in battle with the forces of evil, but also the forces of lawlessness; and not a stroke of God's Law will fall (Matt. 11:11-12; 5:18; Luke 16:16-17). The reign of God is both hope, the yearning of the poor and hungry (so Luke 6:20-21), and becoming a reality in the present.

The kingdom of God, the reign of God, is more than God's will for the individual. It is a corporate image. It is about a changed society. It uses the imagery of the prophets about justice and peace. Meals are a common motif in Jesus' visions of its fulfillment. It is not surprising that he likens the announcement of God's reign to an invitation to a banquet (Luke 14:16-24; cf. Matt. 22:1-14; Matt. 8:11-12; Luke 13:28-29). Throughout his ministry meals, whether with toll collectors and sinners, whether now couched in miraculous terms, whether at the last with the symbols of broken bread and poured out wine, are a significant way of representing the hope of the kingdom (Mark 14:25). The meal is a corporate act, an inclusive event, a fellowship and communion. As such it also became the core of Christian celebration, but in its roots it was a celebration of the vision of the kingdom.

What binds future and present together in Jesus' teaching is the sense that history has reached its climax. The great reversal is around the corner. The poor will be lifted up; the mighty put down from their thrones. The first will be last and the last first (Mark 10:31). This thread of change runs through all of Jesus' teaching. Unlike John the Baptist, who understood himself as being in the preparatory stage, Jesus saw what was happening in his own ministry as the beginning of the new reality. In another saying, probably deriving from Q, Jesus rejects speculation about when the reign of God will come into reality by declaring: "the kingdom is in your midst" (Luke 17:20-21). The sense of ur-

gency and immediacy and at the same time the refusal to speculate
about a timetable creates a tension.

After Jesus' death and resurrection the fervency of hope intensi-
fied; the events of Jesus' resurrection and then the pouring out of the
Spirit were read as further evidence that the climax of history had been
reached. Jesus himself was expected to reappear. Paul still expected Jesus' return in his own lifetime. Jesus left such loose ends, and it became the task of the early Christian communities to work through the
implications.

Jesus' Understanding of God

However vague the timetable, and probably deliberately so, the hope
of God's impending reign was a centerpiece of Jesus' teaching. It inte-
grates all that he said and did. It was also therefore the basis for his understanding of Israel's religious tradition and of their Scripture in particular. Yet it cannot be appreciated without the second key element to
Jesus' thought: his understanding of God. It is one thing to speak of
reign or government; it is quite another thing to ask what kind of government. What kind of God is the God of Jesus? The God of Jesus is
the God of compassion. This theology underlies most of what he says.
It justifies his critique of religious leaders who fail to act compassionately and interpret scriptural law compassionately. It shapes his hope
for the future: wholeness and healing. It explains his willingness to be
imprecise with regard to future events; he can trust God for the future.
It controls his ethic: love of one's enemy. It is the basis of his encour-
agement of trust in daily life. It is the reason for the absence of preoccupation with fulfilling detailed requirements of each and every law,
because the model of God is primarily personal rather than imper-
sonal and legal. It explains his priorities: meeting human need has a
higher priority than fulfilling cultic prescriptions.

Cultic prescriptions are a sticking point. Why single them out, as if
to suggest that they do not belong to love for God and, given the implications of living in a society that needs boundaries, love of one's

neighbor? Is tithing not a structure for maintaining a system given by God for all Israel? Are rites for purification not a way of dealing with dangers for oneself and others? Jesus appears to have sat lightly to such demands, while not repudiating them. They were part of his world, his religion. His initial stance towards lepers, to women who were unclean, to non-Jews, reflects this world; but, even then, what drove him was a higher priority: people's need. More significantly, the understanding of this need reflected a value system that appears to have been developing a distinction between cultic and ethical; not an antithesis, but a differential weighting. One wonders whether exposure to the diverse cultural experience of Galilee, even if from the fringe, contributed to Jesus' willingness to relativize what could be seen as the particulars of his own culture and affirm the universal values of human need and ethics.

I want to suggest that in Jesus we see a style of theology. It is essentially theocentric; God's reign is what matters. It also derives from a particular understanding of God. God is primarily compassionate, and concerned with human well-being. Human well-being is understood primarily in terms of relationships and community. In this the priority is given to the ethical above the cultic. The theology of Jesus is also focused on hope, a vision of fulfillment where such concerns become reality. God will reign; the poor and hungry will no longer be forgotten; people will come together who have not been deemed to belong. This theology is the basis for Jesus' interpretation and reinterpretation of his own religion, including his attitude towards Scripture. It is an inclusive stance. The Scripture and its laws are affirmed; but within them there is a clear focus, a hierarchy of values.

Jesus and Israel

Yet this theology still belongs within a particular religious setting. It is strongly Jewish. The vision of God's reign primarily has Israel in mind. It is Israel's poor who are addressed. These are the poor to whom the good news is preached by the one anointed by the Spirit. The dream

envisages twelve disciples administering the new order of the twelve
tribes from twelve thrones (Luke 22:28:30; Matt. 19:28). Jerusalem is
the dream city and will be the center of the new reality. Gentiles are in
view, at most, on the margins, perhaps under the images of birds nest-
ing in the great tree (Luke 13:18-19; cf. Matt. 13:31-32; Mark 4:30-32).

In Q's community there appears to be a growing sensitivity to the
response of Gentiles to the gospel, so that what were once perhaps references to the gathering of Jews scattered abroad (Q 13:28-29; Matt.
8:11-12) might now include Gentiles. Earlier the focus was primarily
on inclusion of the excluded sons and daughters of Abraham. We see
this in the tradition Luke preserves about the repentance of Zacchaeus
(Luke 19:1-10). Why should he be included? Jesus explains: because
he too is a son of Abraham. Originally the uninvited who fill the banquet hall (Luke 14:16-24; Matt. 22:1-14) would have been the excluded of Israel. The lazy servant wasting the opportunity to invest the
master's money (Matt. 25:14-30; Luke 19:11-27) would have been the
religious authorities of the day.

Even in Q the focus appears to remain within Israel. The bound-
ary-bursting implications of Jesus' inclusive message do not appear to
have broken in on the community, as they had in Mark's community.
This probably reflects a strongly Jewish setting for the communities
that produced Q. We have already noted that much of Jesus' instruction to the crowds has become in Q instruction for the disciples. Similarly, Jesus' conflicts with the religious authorities now reflect conflicts
between the Q community and the religious authorities. Q has extensive material that reflects on conflict and the challenges of being a disciple. Families will have been torn apart; there will have been persecu-
tions; lives will have been lost.

Q has no account of Jesus' death, but it certainly includes material
about Jesus' conflicts. The controversy was sharp and bitter. Jesus attacks the religious leaders for failing in their handling of the religious
tradition of which they were bearers. Failure to give highest priority to
justice and God's love amounted to betrayal of the tradition. Obses-
sion with minutiae had blinded interpreters to the major demands of
the Bible. Like Mark, Q reports the accusation made against Jesus by

the religious teachers of the day — that he was in league with Beelzebub. The conflict had escalated into one between good and evil in absolute terms. John's warnings about the judgment day find their echo in the teachings of Jesus, who declares the frightening obverse of his message of radical inclusion; those who resent it and by their interpretation and behavior block it will themselves face exclusion at the last.

Conflict over the Scriptures

Yet what was at stake? This was a conflict about how to interpret the Bible by two groups, both of whom affirmed it in its entirety. It was not a conflict between believers and unbelievers, but within the context of Israel's religion, between believers. It was not a conflict even between which parts of the Bible to believe and which to set aside, as it might have been with Mark and Paul, but between people who affirmed the whole. The point has often been made that the heat of the controversy probably reflects the fact that both sides belong closely together. There is no evidence that Jesus was a Pharisee, but by his background and general religious stance, he clearly had much in common with them. On the other side, examination of the earliest material prevents a wholesale identification of Jesus' opponents as Pharisees, though doubtless some of them belonged to their more extreme adherents.

When we stand back and look at the ferocity of this dispute, it should not surprise us to find similar heat in the conflict over interpreting the Bible today. I am not suggesting that we emulate the threats and censures that this controversy evoked. But I do believe we need to take seriously the way that dispute over how to approach the Bible takes us onto familiar ground. Jesus and his first followers, even those of the more conservative mold, such as those represented in the Q material, put their lives on the line for an interpretation that brought to the Scriptures a hierarchy of values which they claimed the Scriptures themselves generated: that people matter most to God; that God is compassionate; that wholeness and restoration of community are the top priority; that these matter more than observance of ritual and cultic minutiae. God is not the great egotist who wants everything done his way for his sake without concern for people, but the God of compassion for whom the tradition of biblical instruction is the vestige of continuing care and love that can continue to be read from real-life experience. The power is not in those who hold the book and administer its law, but in love that finds expression also in human families and the world of nature. Such love does not depend on deriving its authority from the Bible; Jesus rarely taught this way. Rather, he restates what is at the heart of Scripture.

These are daring thoughts and immensely frustrating to those who want the lines of authority more clearly defined. The pressure was mounting on the Q community, which was probably very glad to reaffirm its master's commitment to maintaining every stroke of the Law. In time, the forces of control would establish Jesus in his place as a definable authority, although this authority would still be difficult to maintain. It would be easier to replace him by the written word and to reinvent a fundamentalism that gave greater security. As each generation faces afresh the issue of how then to approach this word, the storms begin anew.

• 4 •

MATTHEW

Radical Obedience to God's Law

When we come to Matthew we are dealing with a gospel that has combined both Mark and Q as well as adding other independent material. We have seen that Q represents a strong statement about upholding the Law; not a stroke will fall. We have also seen that for Mark not just a stroke but large sections of the Law had to fall to removes obstacles to the inclusion of Gentiles in the people of God. How could one possibly combine two such divergent approaches?

The answer lies partly in noting what both Q and Mark have in common: both represent Jesus as having an attitude towards Scripture and its commandments which reflected certain priorities. People mattered most, not laws; ethical attitude and behavior mattered more than fulfilling cultic and ritual requirements. The difference was particularly about the extent to which this priority subordinated the other or, as in Mark, was ground for its exclusion. In addition, both portray the magnetic effects of hope and of the person of Jesus. The vision of hope and of the values it enshrines becomes a point of reference for what matters already in living here and now. Jesus himself also becomes a point of reference for what is authoritative. In both, therefore, the focus of authority is no longer written Scripture alone, but a person and a vision. They vary in the implications of this new development of thought.

The Beginning

The most striking thing, when we turn to Matthew — indeed for any-
one who thinks to read the New Testament for the first time — is that
it begins with a long list of names, a genealogy setting out Jesus' forebears on his father's side, or, at least, his so-called father's side. It is just
like the lists of forebears we come across in the Old Testament, and in
part is based on them. At a number of levels this tells us a lot about
Matthew's attitude towards Scripture. To begin with, the list secures an
actual connection between the story of Jesus and the stories of Scripture. The form of the genealogy makes the story of Jesus sound like
Scripture, and this would certainly be Matthew's intention: Jesus' story
is also sacred story. In that sense Matthew is writing Scripture, with
echoes both in form and content of the Scripture of old. His frequent
editorial additions of "and behold" to stories from Mark exemplify
this trend, but so does much else. The genealogy is also more than a
list; it is stylized: broken into three sections, each with fourteen generations, a pattern of three fourteens (or six sevens), figures designed to
reinforce the claim that the story Matthew is about to unfold belongs
to careful divine planning and represents fulfillment of Scripture's
hopes.

This latter feature, fulfillment of the hopes of Scripture, is a consistent theme in Matthew. "This was to fulfill that which was spoken by
the prophet saying" regularly introduces a reference to such predictions. Only Matthew has the stories of Joseph's dream and of the magi
and Herod. Throughout these first two chapters about Jesus' birth and
infancy we find not only direct reference to fulfillment of Scripture,
but elaborate echoes of Old Testament stories. There are echoes of familiar stories: the plight of the little child Moses, the journey of Israel
to Egypt and the exodus, the confrontation with the wicked king Balak
and Balaam's prediction of a star.

In setting the scene at the beginning of his gospel Matthew is es-
tablishing the basis for what is to follow. He is also revealing to us his
own stance concerning Jesus and the Scripture. In this he goes far beyond what we have found in Mark or Q in showing that what hap-

pened in Jesus happened in accordance with Scripture. This sense of
continuity receives maximum attention and comes to expression not
only in what is said but in the way it is said. Q had emphasized that
the Law of Scripture remained valid. Matthew goes far beyond this. At
every opportunity he underlines the scripturalness of the story of Jesus.
Jesus is not only in conflict with scribes; he is, in the best sense, a
scribe himself. Thus Matthew ends the Sermon on the Mount with the
note that the people were astonished at Jesus' authority because he
taught with authority and not as their scribes. On another occasion he
has Jesus speak of the true Christian teacher as a scribe and speaks of
God's wisdom sending apostles and scribes to the people of Israel
(13:52). Matthew's approach is scribal. It is scribal in the sense that it
regularly seeks to explain the story of Jesus in terms that prove his legitimacy on the basis of Scripture. He has moved from portraying Jesus
as a teacher of wisdom whose teaching can be seen in the broadest
sense as an exposition of God's will and therefore upholding God's
Law — the stance of Q — to portraying him as an expositor of Scripture in the scribal tradition.

We see this in the contrast between Jesus' statements about divorce, retaliation, and treatment of one's enemy in Q and the way they
now appear in Matthew. In Q Jesus makes statements about each of
these, but without a specific link to Scripture. In Matthew they have
been taken up into a group of six statements introduced by a statement
from Scripture: "You have heard that it was said." Jesus' words take up
what is said in Scripture and expound it differently from the way many
had been understanding it. The issue is how to interpret Scripture. We
shall return to these in more detail below.

The same sense of identity between Jesus and Scripture, especially
what Scripture commands in the Law, is to be found in that remarkable passage where Jesus cries out, "Come to me all who labor and are
heavy laden and I will give you rest; take my yoke upon you and learn
of me, for I am meek and lowly of heart, and you shall find rest for
your souls, for my yoke is easy and my burden is light" (Matt. 11:28-
30). It comes as the climax of an interesting sequence of statements
drawn from Q. First both John and Jesus are portrayed as envoys of

God's wisdom. Then Jesus gives thanks that he has been able to pass on wisdom to his disciples. There follows the statement about Jesus' unique authority, which is based on a unique relationship between himself and God, a mutual knowing. Then come Jesus' words of invitation which I have quoted. The call to take upon oneself God's yoke is a familiar image in Judaism. It is the call to take onto oneself the yoke of God's Law. Sometimes people spoke of God's Law or Word in very personal terms as God's Wisdom. Wisdom invites. Frequently Wisdom is pictured as a woman, as in Proverbs. Wisdom acts on God's behalf. Here in Matthew Jesus acts as God's Wisdom, summoning people to take on the yoke of God's Law. In other words, for Matthew, Jesus is not only teaching in a way that alters no stroke of the Law; he is proclaiming God's Law and expounding it. The yoke of the Law, expounded by Jesus, is not burdensome, because he brings to Scripture his distinctive approach which makes the Law work for people — as was intended — not make people work for the Law.

We shall return later to the distinctive way that Jesus interprets the Law in Matthew; our main point here is to show what Matthew is doing. Far from setting Jesus and his authority in contrast with that of the Law of Scripture he brings them inseparably together, so that Jesus becomes the Law's chief exponent. Continuity and consistency is a hallmark of Matthew's presentation of this relationship.

John and Jesus and the Disciples

Another area where this is particularly clear is in the way Matthew portrays the ministries of John the Baptist, Jesus, and the disciples. In portraying the appearance of John the Baptist, Matthew combines material from Q and Mark. Both present John as calling people to repent. It is the material from Q that provides the substance for John's preaching. As we have seen, John calls for change. People should not assume that being children of Abraham will indemnify them against God's judgment. The only thing that will indemnify them against God's judgment will be submission to God's Law and baptism, which represents that submission and God's cleansing forgiveness. John speaks of submission to God's Law as bearing good fruit, the fruit of good deeds. The alternative is to face fiery judgment.

Matthew takes over all of this, but he adds a new beginning. John's first words are: "Repent, the kingdom of heaven is at hand" (3:2). These are also the words that summarize Jesus' preaching in 4:17 and the disciples' preaching in 10:7. Matthew has taken what he found as a summary of Jesus' preaching in Mark 1:15 and made it also the summary of John's preaching. The variations in wording are insignificant: "kingdom of heaven" is Matthew's preferred term rather than "kingdom of God." By "heaven" Matthew means God. The effect of this transfer of Jesus' message onto the lips of John is twofold. First, it has the effect of using John's preaching as the first definition of the kingdom. The message of the kingdom is, therefore, the challenge to take on the yoke of God's Law, to change one's life, to become obedient, to bear fruit, to submit to what Scripture demands.

The second effect is to underline that John, Jesus, and the disciples belong closely together. We find the same thing happening again in the closing chapters which depict Jesus' ministry. In 21:23-27 Matthew reports the question raised by the chief priests and the elders of the people about Jesus' authority. At this point Matthew is using Mark as his source. As in Mark, Matthew tells us that Jesus responded to their question by asking them first to indicate what they thought about John's authority. That stumped them.

Matthew then expands this link between Jesus' authority and John's authority by stringing together three parables, only one of which he found in Mark. The first illustrates rejection of John; the second illustrates rejection of Jesus himself; the third illustrates rejection of Jesus' disciples. They are the parable of the two sons (21:28-31), one declaring he would do his father's will and then failing to do so and the other doing the reverse. To this parable Matthew adds as a word of Jesus: "For John came to you in the way of righteousness and you did not believe him, but the toll collectors and the prostitutes believed him; but you when you saw this did not later repent and believe him" (21:32).

The second parable is the one that Matthew found in Mark, about the wicked vineyard workers who refused to deliver produce to the owner and even killed his beloved Son (21:33-46). The third is the parable of the wedding feast, which interprets the destruction of Jerusalem as God's judgment on the leaders of Jerusalem for rejecting the gospel (22:1-14). Thus just as all three — John, Jesus, and the disciples — preach the same message, so all three face the same kind of rejection.

Jesus — Israel's Messiah and Son of God

It is not that Matthew puts them all at the same level. Clearly Jesus towers above both John and the disciples, but he does so as the one who is uniquely authorized to expound God's Law. He does so as Israel's Messiah and as the uniquely created Son of God who bears the Spirit. The difference and the similarity come through strongly at Jesus' baptism by John. First, John is reluctant to baptize his superior. Then Jesus declares that it is necessary to fulfill all righteousness. In this case the reference is not to fulfillment of a scriptural command, but nevertheless to what Jesus sees as God's will. And by putting it in this way, "We must fulfill all righteousness," Matthew is showing us again that this is the central concern both for Jesus and for everyone else, including John. It is interesting that later, as we have just seen, Matthew describes John as coming "in the way of righteousness." "Righteousness" is a key theme in Matthew, precisely because it expresses this total commitment to doing God's will as set forth in Scripture and elsewhere.

In Matthew's version of the baptism of Jesus, the words from on high take on new meaning in the light of this emphasis. For a start, they are directed not to Jesus but to everyone present, and by extension, also to the hearers of the Gospel of Matthew in every age, including ourselves. They reinforce the understanding that Jesus is the Son of God divinely created through Mary. The words, "In whom I am well pleased," also reflect on Jesus' determined commitment to total obedience, shown in the encounter with John. As in Q, the temptation narrative that follows cements this impression. Jesus is the Son of God who upholds God's Law and appeals to it as the basis for his action.

The Sermon on the Mount

This brings us to the Sermon on the Mount where, above all, we find the distinctive emphasis of Matthew coming through strongly. We have already noted that it ends with a contrast between Jesus and "their scribes." We have also seen that what in Q was teaching only very indirectly related to Scripture becomes scribal exposition of Scripture. Now we can move to 5:17-20, where Jesus addresses the legitimacy of Scripture and its law directly. Before we do, however, it is important not to overlook that the Sermon on the Mount begins with the so-called beatitudes (5:3-12). In other words, before addressing the commands of Scripture, Jesus addresses the hopes of the kingdom. These come to us in Matthew as an extensive expansion of what was in Q. Instead of four promises of blessing we have nine. It appears that even before Matthew the Q version had undergone expansion.

The first eight fall into two neat groups of four. The first and the eighth promise the kingdom of heaven: "Blessed are the poor in spirit, for theirs is the kingdom of heaven" (5:3); "Blessed are those persecuted for the sake of righteousness, for theirs is the kingdom of heaven" (5:10). Similarly the fourth and the eighth, ending each section, refer to "righteousness." We have just quoted the eighth; the fourth reads: "Blessed are those who hunger and thirst for righteousness, for they shall be satisfied" (5:6). The ninth, which is taken from Q, keeps the form it had in Q, so that instead of saying "Blessed are those who" it says, "Blessed are you when people despise and persecute you and speak all manner of evil against you" (5:11-12).

Perhaps all of this reflects Matthew's careful composition. The result is that the blessings fall into three groups of three; Matthew loves threes. But it is also that the blessings reflect more strongly what Matthew sees as the heart of Jesus' message. The key expressions, "kingdom of heaven" and "righteousness" receive double emphasis. In addition, while some remain promises to the needy (those who mourn, those who are persecuted), the emphasis falls on those who do what is right: "are gentle, merciful, pure in heart, and peacemakers." Those described as "poor in spirit" and "hungering and thirsting for righteousness or justice" are probably also people exhibiting lowliness and a desire for righteousness in their attitudes and actions, though they may include people in need. The overall effect of the blessings in Matthew, however, is that they encourage commitment to keeping God's Law. At the same time they also give important clues about where the priorities are for Matthew when it comes to applying the Scripture and its Law. This is very important.

Already in the first chapter of the gospel, Matthew tells us that Joseph was a righteous person (1:19). That meant that he was committed to keeping God's Law as set out in Scripture relating to women who fell pregnant out of wedlock to someone other than their fiancé. But it also meant that in applying the options Joseph chose the more compassionate alternative. He chose not to take her to court, but to deal with the matter in privacy. The same emphasis on compassion runs throughout the blessings, so that righteousness and purity of heart must be understood in terms of mercy, gentleness, and peacemaking. The exhortations that follow, about being salt and light in the world, build on this understanding. This is very important as we approach Jesus' major statements about the Law in 5:17-20 and then consider their application to specific areas in what follows.

Jesus and the Law

Matthew makes unmistakably plain in 5:17 that Jesus has no intention of undermining Scripture, represented here as the Law and the Prophets: "Do not think that I have come to annul the Law and the Prophets; I have not come to annul them but to fulfil them." Who could have ever thought otherwise? Perhaps some who had read Mark might have thought so. Perhaps Jews were accusing Matthew and his community of doing so. To Matthew's mind this is completely wrong. On the contrary, Jesus came to fulfill the Scriptures. That has two aspects which belong together under the general notion of making sure what they say is done. That will include fulfilling predictions, an important theme in Matthew; it also includes doing what is demanded and making sure it is done rightly.

Next, Matthew produces a revised version of a saying we noted in Q, where it spoke of it being harder for heaven and earth to pass away than for a stroke of the Law to fall. Matthew's version reads: "Truly I tell you, until heaven and earth pass away, not a jot not a stroke of the Law will pass away, until all is done" (5:18). It is a complete misreading of this to suggest that Matthew is saying that the Law is only temporary until the end of time, let alone until the time of Jesus' death and resurrection. The point about heaven and earth passing away is just a very strong way of saying: never! In no way can God's Law be annulled, not a single part of it! The thought is not dissimilar to 24:35: "Heaven and earth will pass away, but my words shall not pass away." "Until all is done" simply reinforces the issue. It is not preserving the Law intact so much as making sure it is done, making sure it reaches fulfillment in behavior.

The next verse reinforces this demand: "Whoever breaks one of these least commandments and teaches people to do so shall be called least in the kingdom of heaven; whoever does them and teaches them, shall be called great in the kingdom of heaven" (5:19). This may be just a rhetorical way of saying there is no place in God's community for people who disobey and teach people to disobey God's Law. It is certainly interesting, because it implies that some people do teach disobedience to the Law. Would Matthew have interpreted Mark's stance in this way? Mark does, after all, say that Jesus annulled large sections of biblical law. But if Matthew had such a low view of Mark, it is unlikely he would have made such extensive use of his account, unless, perhaps, he felt it was in part correct. Paul comes into the same category. Did Matthew know of his work?

Perhaps we have to be satisfied with noting that Matthew must have seen some people as engaging in such teaching. In 24:11-12 he mentions false prophets who will lead people astray to wickedness (perhaps lawlessness in the sense of direct flouting of the Law, although this is uncertain). The result will be a failure of love; that fits Matthew's emphasis. Such concern also seems to be reflected in the final sections of the Sermon on the Mount, which gives extensive attention to false prophets and their failure to bear good fruit, a theme addressed identically by John (7:15-20). He also mentions people claiming allegiance to Jesus as Lord and performing miraculous works in his name, but failing to bear such fruit (7:21-23). Such situations may have motivated the strong disclaimer already in 5:17, that Jesus did not come to annul the Law.

5:19 is also fascinating when read more literally as a comment about the status of people within the kingdom of heaven. People who are called least in the kingdom of heaven are nevertheless still in it. It is likely, then, that Matthew is telling us that Jesus has something to say about the different approaches taken to the Law within early Christianity, and he comes down firmly on the side of a strict observance of the Law, rather than modifying it, let alone annulling it. This might make better sense of Matthew's taking up Mark's account while disagreeing with it at certain points.

5:20 reflects the other group about whom Matthew is so sensitive — the scribes and Pharisees: "For I tell you that unless your righteousness exceeds that of the scribes and the Pharisees, you shall not enter the kingdom of heaven." It is not only a matter of rejecting new Christian modifications of the Law; it is a matter of obedience that has to be a lot better than the kind shown by those who are the champions of the Law in Judaism.

Contrasted Ways of Hearing Scripture

This then sets the scene for the teaching that follows, in which Jesus contrasts his own interpretation of the commandments with the way they were interpreted at least at a popular level by some. It is here that we find what kind of thing drove Jesus' approach to Scripture, as Matthew sees it. Already the selection of themes tells us something. There is nothing here about purity laws, or matters referring to food preparation, and only indirectly a reference to the temple. Matters of a broadly cultic character appear in 6:1-18. The focus of the six contrasts is primarily on attitudes and behavior in human relationships.

The first of these contrasts shifts the emphasis from the command not to murder to the demand that people should not be murderous and hateful in their attitudes (5:21-22). Such anger is the antithesis of love. It is mistaken to interpret Matthew as attacking an emotion as such; his Jesus is also angry at times. The focus is an attitude that easily emerges from the emotion and is even to be seen in verbal assaults. Matthew is not interested just in intentions and interior dispositions, but in attitude and behavior. That is evident in the instruction about being a blessed peacemaker, sorting out conflict issues that people have with you before bringing your offering to the temple (5:23-24). Notice that this is an inclusive priority. That is, it does not assume that peacemaking removes the need to bring the offering; you do both. Only, make sure you settle the one first before doing the other.

The second contrast is similar to the first. It shifts the focus from acts of adultery to adulterous attitudes (5:27-28). Again, Matthew probably does not intend to portray Jesus as outlawing sexual feelings; it is a matter of what we do with them in attitude and behavior. The words that follow, about cutting off an offending hand (5:29-30), are dramatic and intended to underline that the matter is to be taken with utmost seriousness. In this and the previous contrast the underlying value is on the person; here, the woman. People matter. Love and respect inform the way scriptural law is interpreted. It takes us far further than a literal approach would. This needs to be underlined because many people see the contrast between the spirit and the letter as implying that the way of the spirit leads to greater leniency; not so, here.

Jesus' words about divorce take us in a similar direction of greater strictness (5:31-32). They doubtless reflect the belief that such a provision is being abused. Matthew's Jewish community context is reflected in the fact that both here and later in 19:9 Matthew has rewritten the saying (cf. Mark 10:11-12; Luke 16:18) so that it reflects biblical law, according to which only the man could divorce. Matthew has also modified his tradition to bring it more directly into line with the biblical provision: divorce only on grounds of immorality. Unfortunately this has had the effect in subsequent history of putting all the emphasis on the act of adultery again, quite contrary to the spirit of the previous contrast, which was moving away from that kind of thinking.

The fourth contrast has Jesus forbid oaths altogether (5:33-37). People of the time would have understood this not as undermining the Law, which does, under certain circumstances, allow for oaths, but as applying it even more strictly. A very literal, mathematically logical approach results in the conclusion that at this point Jesus annuls part of the Law and so contradicts himself. But this misses the point. The point is that all manipulative verbal behavior is being outlawed. That is in accord with the emphasis in Scripture on truth. It is interesting that in this section the argument is made with reference to the concerns of the Jew, including the Christian Jew, and in traditional Jewish terms: "Do not swear at all; neither by heaven, for it is God's throne; nor by earth, because it is his footstool, nor by Jerusalem, for it is the city of the great king." Finally only a straight "Yes, yes" or "no, no" is allowed, something later generations will see as still a form of oath (2 Enoch 49:10).

This fourth contrast enables us to identify an important distinction in approaches to Scripture. An approach that looks primarily at the letter of the Scripture must acknowledge a contradiction in Matthew or somehow explain away one or other side of it. In fact, the surface contradiction points to the fact that Matthew's approach is not literal in this sense. The statement about not one stroke falling must be seen not as literal but rhetorical. That is, it is a strong affirmation of the Law's continuing validity. That validity will not be measured at a literal level by the presence or absence of strokes of letters or even the detail of particular commandments, but on upholding what is the Law's underlying demand. Doing this will at times far exceed what is written; on occasions, superficially, it will differ from what is specified. The overall direction is one of upholding the Law, not undermining it.

This is an important distinction because, for all Matthew's insistence on the Law and making its demands central to the gospel, he is not a literalist. He approaches Scripture on the basis of an understanding of what matters most within it and what is the intention of its particular commands. This is still, however, a long way from an approach that then uses a general understanding of the Law's intention to remove large slabs of what is commanded, such as we find in Mark.

The final two contrasts (5:38-48) pick up and expand teachings of Jesus found in Q but set them now in the context of the Law. What Jesus is attacking here is not the justice system that operates on a principle of precise restitution, but the abuse of this system in personal relations to justify hatred and violence. In these sections which have in mind also exploitative relations and situations of persecution, Jesus instructs the disciples to respond not with violence but peaceably. The thread that links the instructions together is love and respect for other human beings, and this flows in turn from a theology that portrays God as merciful and compassionate to all without discrimination. When the chapter ends with the demand to be perfect like God, it is this kind of perfection that Matthew has in mind. It is the purity of heart, praised in the blessing, which is gentle, merciful, and peacemaking. Such also is the righteousness to be sought after and to stand up for, which exceeds that of the scribes and Pharisees.

The upshot of this discussion is that while Matthew (of all the gospels) insists on the harmony between the authority of Jesus and that of Scripture, it is on the basis of an approach to Scripture that is not superficial — an approach that demands compliance to the letter but goes beyond the letter. It is always in the direction of greater demand. Even in the one instance where it effectively removes a literal provision, it does so in the direction not of greater leniency but greater strictness. At the same time this greater strictness lies not in the multiplication of commands or of the application of commands to particular situations, but in an integrative approach that looks at commands in the light of principles which are seen to underlie them or should underlie them. These find their basis in an understanding of God as compassionate and caring towards all human beings, without discrimination.

Compassion and Caring for People

It is this thread of compassion and caring for people which indirectly also underlies the attack in 6:1-18 on hypocrisy, seen as the attempt to manipulate others by false appearances or putting on a show. Matthew places this discussion of giving to charity through the temple system, of prayer and fasting, under the heading of righteousness. It looks very much as though these have developed their own distinctively Christian forms by the time Matthew is writing, but they belong in general to the Jewish piety of the time. The centerpiece is prayer, and here Matthew has placed an expanded form of the Lord's Prayer, found in a shorter version in Q. It stands directly beside a statement about forgiveness of others, reinforcing one of its petitions; it is echoed by Matthew's emphasis on restored relationships, mercy, and peacemaking.

In the rest of Matthew 6 Jesus warns about greed. In contrast he encourages the disciples to approach basic human needs like food and shelter and clothing with trust, and he assumes a community of faith in which such needs can be met. A community where people seek first God's kingdom as well as pray for it to come is liable to be such a community. It will also be one where destructive criticism is absent and where needs can be met. As in Q, Matthew follows such exhortation by the so-called golden rule, that one should treat others as one would want to be treated by others. It is typical of Matthew that he adds: "For this is the Law and the Prophets." Such a statement would be outrageous to someone who saw upholding the temple worship as the highest priority; it could at most be a reasonable summary of some of the Law and the Prophets. But here we again see Matthew's orientation.

From 7:15-22 we have the warnings about false prophets and Christians who acclaim Jesus as Lord but do not keep his commands. The Sermon on the Mount ends with the famous parable about building on sand or on rock. For Matthew, to build on the rock is to uphold the Law and the Prophets as interpreted by Jesus. That was John's demand. That is Jesus' demand. That will be the message of the disciples. That is what it means to pray, "Your kingdom come."

"Not as Their Scribes"

We return then to Matthew's final comment after the Sermon. People were astonished at Jesus' teaching, "because he was teaching them as one who had authority, and not as their scribes." It is worth pausing over this comment. Matthew has taken it out of Mark's story about Jesus in the synagogue (Mark 1:21-28). This is one of the few anecdotes from Mark that Matthew does not include. In Mark it ended with the crowd acclaiming: "What is this? A new teaching with authority" (Mark 1:27). For Matthew, Jesus' teaching is not so much new teaching as an exposition of the established authority of the Scriptures. Yet Matthew is obviously one with Mark in emphasizing Jesus' authority. He endorses Mark's emphasis and expands it. As we have already noted, he transforms the baptism into a more public event. He introduces it with two chapters that inextricably bind the story of Jesus to sacred story of old and provide a new basis for explaining Jesus' authority.

Yet this authority is seen differently from in Mark. It is absolute authority under God, but much more strongly identified with the authority of Scripture and much more closely identified with the authority of the church. I have already illustrated the identification with the authority of Scripture. It occurs throughout Matthew. For instance, in retelling the controversy over eating with toll collectors and sinners, Matthew adds as a word of Jesus: "Go and learn what this means, 'I desire mercy and not sacrifice'" (9:13a). Matthew adds the identical passage into the controversy about plucking grain on the sabbath (12:7). There he also includes what we would have to describe as scribal argument to justify Jesus' stance: priests work on the sabbath. In that context he even omits what was probably Jesus' original reply, "The sabbath was made for people, not people for the sabbath" (Mark 2:27), because he prefers always to link justification either to Scripture or to Jesus as authorities. He rewrites the story of the healing of the man with the withered hand on the sabbath so that it now becomes more directly a legal argument about the application of biblical sabbath law, and he has Jesus engage in a bit of case law (12:9-14).

Jesus' Authority and the Church's Authority

We can see that Matthew also relates Jesus' authority (and in this sense also Scripture's authority) to that of the church. Many have noted the telling way that Matthew concludes his highly abbreviated account of Jesus' healing of a paralyzed man, the one who according to Mark was let down through the roof, a detail Matthew drops (9:2-8; cf. Mark 2:1-12). Matthew explains that the crowd were amazed that God had given such authority to human beings (9:8). We have already noted the way Jesus, John, and the disciples share the same message. The disciples share the same message because Jesus has authorized them to teach and preach.

Matthew highlights this authority especially through the figure of Peter. In an extraordinarily creative expansion of the account of Jesus' walking on the water, Matthew has Peter also invited to take the same steps (Matt. 14:22-33; cf. Mark 6:46-52). The symbolism would not be lost in a culture that often spoke of the deep as the powers that overwhelm. The incident finds its echo when Jesus declares that Peter, whose name means the rock or stone, will be the rock on which the church is to be built (16:16-19). The powers of the underworld will not overwhelm it. In this context Jesus gives Peter the keys and the authority to bind and loose. Two chapters later, in the context of discipline within the community, Jesus again speaks of this authority (18:18-20). Here it is given to the church meeting in the spiritual presence of Jesus to rule on matters of law. Clearly Peter's role is representative of this role given to the church and exercised especially by people like Matthew, but also by other faithful disciples in the community.

The language and the functions echo those of the scribes. It is not so easy to determine whether binding and loosing refers to teaching or to determination of law. From a normal scribal perspective, which we may assume, I think, for Matthew, it means both. For Scripture interpretation is about determining how Scripture applies to life situations. In this, according to Matthew, Jesus has given authority to the church. Interpreting Scripture is not a private matter, but belongs within the context of the community. This is an important insight for viewing the handling of Scripture in our own day.

The gospel of Matthew ends with Jesus' great commission to his disciples (28:16-20). Again, the typically Matthean emphases are present. Even the presence of Jesus on a high mountain evokes the biblical story, especially the image of Sinai and perhaps Zion, from which the Law will go forth to the nations. Authorization is the language. Jesus has received all authority. In a sense that is nothing new; but Matthew is not thinking in abstract terms. According to 11:27 the Father had given him "all things," but this related to his authority to teach. The authority here is related to the extent of the mission to follow. It had been restricted to Israel; it is now to go to all nations.

The mission is a teaching one expressed in making disciples and teaching them all that Jesus had commanded them. Note the emphasis on the gospel as demand, as it had been from the beginning with John. Though not explicitly stated, it is about proclaiming the demand of God's will, set forth in Scripture, in the Law and the Prophets and expounded by Jesus. And just as in Jewish tradition, God's Shekinah, God's presence, was promised where two or three gathered to study the Law, so here Jesus promises his presence among his disciples as they embark on their mission of teaching.

They will baptize as did John, but now in the name, not of John, but of Jesus. The threefold form is not so much trinitarian as it is a formulation that picks up important aspects of theology: God authorizes the baptism; it is in the light of Jesus' exposition of God's will; through it the Spirit will be given, just as Jesus received the Spirit in the context of his baptism.

The Law and the Gentiles: Undoing Mark

There is one thing evoked by this mission charge which we have passed over until now. What will be the effect of this mission to all nations on the way people should treat the Law? After all, that was the burning issue with which Paul grappled and which is reflected in

Mark. Does Matthew, who espouses such total commitment to the Scripture and its Law, envisage that these new Gentile converts will undergo circumcision and keep food laws?

The issue where we might expect the matter to come through in Matthew is at the point where he takes up those central chapters in Mark that deal with food laws in the context of celebrating the inclusion of Gentiles in the people of God (Mark 6–8). We recall that Mark used the two feeding miracles of the five thousand and the four thousand within a larger composition to highlight the fact that in Jesus both Jews and Gentiles receive the nourishment of the gospel. The first is colored with imagery suggestive of Israel and takes place in Jewish territory; the second takes place in Gentile territory and is without the distinctive traces of the former. Between these miracles at the center of the composition is the controversy with scribes and Pharisees about washing hands, which becomes a discussion of clean and unclean foods and concludes by declaring that Jesus effectively declared such laws invalid. For nothing from outside a person can matter in that way. Mark had attached to this controversy the anecdote about Jesus' encounter with a Syrophoenician woman, which showed Jesus moving from a position of discrimination (she is a dog; Jews are children) to one of inclusion. Mark draws attention to the message of his composition in 8:16-21 and bemoans the failure of the disciples to see the point.

Matthew also has the same material in the same sequence as in Mark, but with striking transformations. Gone is much of the Jewish imagery from the feeding of the five thousand (14:13-21; cf. Mark 6:32-44). It is clearly still a Jewish crowd. But now so is the crowd of four thousand (15:29-39; cf. Mark 8:1-10). The anecdote has been reshaped to reflect fulfillment of the prophetic tradition about healing and feeding on Mount Zion at the end of time. The discussion between Jesus and his disciples about the miracles no longer focuses on numeric symbolism (16:5-12; cf. Mark 8:16-21).

The centerpiece has also been rewritten (15:1-20; cf. Mark 7:1-23). No longer does it support the conclusion that Jesus declared food or purity laws invalid; Mark's addition to this effect is deleted (Mark

7:19). Instead, the episode amounts to an attack on an extremist demand about hand washing and leaves food laws and the like untouched. Inner purity and ethics still receive highest priority but not at the expense of other laws. All hint of ridicule and disparagement of concern with externals has gone.

The encounter with the Syrophoenician woman becomes stereotypically a meeting with a Canaanite (15:21-28; cf. Mark 7:24-30). The sharp discrimination remains; the woman makes three appeals, not one. But in the context of doing so she offers a model of the faith that Israel should show, hailing Jesus as Son of David. She is an exception. Jesus reminds her in words added by Matthew, "I was sent only to the lost sheep of the house of Israel" (15:24). This recalls his instructions to his own disciples earlier, that they should work only in Israel and not enter Gentile or Samaritan territory (10:5-6). Like the account of the centurion and his servant (8:5-13), this anecdote serves to shame Israel. But both also point forward to a future expansion of the mission to Gentiles. In the former, Matthew has included the Q saying of Jesus: "Many shall come east and west and shall sit at table with Abraham, Isaac and Jacob in the kingdom of God" (8:11).

As a result we can say that Matthew does not agree with Mark's conclusions about food and purity laws and revises Mark's careful composition to remove such a suggestion. He does however approve of a Gentile mission, but one wonders whether his community really knows it at firsthand. Probably Matthew's situation is such that the issue of whether to drop the demand of circumcision had not arisen or, if it had, had been settled in favor of retention. This is more thinkable in a community still predominantly Jewish. Matthew's strong insistence on a commitment to the demands of the Law and the Prophets without exception may even indicate that so far he disapproves of such exceptions. Yet Matthew's approach to the Scripture and its Law, which made compassion central because compassion was central to its understanding of God, would at least mean that Matthew's community might entertain other options in the future.

Competing in a Jewish Community

Matthew's community finds itself in a strongly Jewish context, but clearly sensing itself as a minority group that did not "call the shots" in the Judaism of its day. It is in conflict with the scribes and the Pharisees, who doubtless represent the dominant authority. Matthew as much as acknowledges this when he has Jesus declare that they "sit on Moses' seat" and are to be obeyed (23:2-3). With his commitment to full observance, such an exhortation makes sense. Matthew's gripe is not the Law they represent but their failure to keep it themselves. As one reads on in Matthew 23 it becomes clear that there is also an issue with the way they impose or apply rulings that Matthew finds restrictive and burdensome. This is the import of Jesus' words that his burden is light. There are just as many commands, but applied from a different perspective.

The attack on his contemporaries takes up material from Q that we have already considered. Matthew is quite comfortable about having Jesus agree to careful tithing even of herbs, provided there is no neglect of "justice and mercy and faith," Matthew's revision of the earlier, "justice and the love of God" (23:23). He is also happy to reaffirm that they have the keys to the kingdom of heaven (23:13); but Peter and Matthew and his community will do a far better job in expounding what these keys are about, the Scripture and its Law, than they do (16:19; 18:18). Matthew is also unimpressed by their Gentile converts (23:15). Perhaps they are particularly zealous opponents of the Christian movement because of its reputation elsewhere. Matthew mocks debates about appropriateness of oaths, but does so in very Jewish terms concerned with altars and sacrifices and aspects of the temple cult (23:16-22). Matthew's version of the saying about washing the inside of cups and plates merges ritual and ethical purity, emphasizing the latter, but not despising the former (23:25-26). Matthew concludes the attack with judgment on Israel's leaders for rejecting the church's prophets, sages, and scribes, and points to the temple's destruction as the fruit of such folly (23:29-39). Against such judgment Matthew, like Q, holds out the hope of a new beginning for Jerusalem with a return of Christ to rule (23:39).

Jesus and the Temple: Undoing Mark

As Matthew wards off Mark's radical solution with regard to purity and food laws, so he removes all suggestion that Jesus disparages the temple. Gone is the description of the temple as only something made with human hands (26:61; cf. Mark 14:58). The false testimony that Jesus would destroy the temple becomes an affirmation that he could destroy it; he will not. Judgment remains. And part of God's judgment will mean the destruction of the temple, but gone is the suggestion that the community of faith is the new temple. Jesus confronts abuses in the temple as a prophet, like Jeremiah in his day (21:10-22). Jesus heals and teaches in the temple. There is no hint of criticism of the temple itself and the biblically sanctioned ordinances that undergird it.

Even the sympathetic scribe's rating of the great commandments above sacrifices has been rewritten to delete the potentially negative references to the cult (22:34-39; cf. Mark 12:28-34). The negative disappears. Only the positive remains. To this Matthew adds that the whole Law and the Prophets hang on these great commandments (22:40); indirectly he is again warding off the slightest hint that Jesus might have spoken against the Law and the Prophets. These still stand, and the key to their understanding is the twofold law of love.

We find the same emphasis in Matthew's interesting revision of Mark's story of Jesus' encounter with a rich man (19:16-22; cf. Mark 10:17-22). In response to the question about eternal life, Jesus does not cite the ethical parts of the ten commandments loosely; he quotes them exactly, deleting what does not occur there and appending the command to love one's neighbor as oneself. Playfully he has changed the conversation partner; the rich man looking back on his own obedience has been replaced by a youth. Matthew has then introduced the term "perfection," not as the *higher* goal but as the *only* goal of faith. Greek listeners would appreciate the play on words: the word for perfection is also the word for maturity. The young man needs to grow up! Instead he turns away. Only perfection matters. For Matthew that is a matter of quality rather than quantity. Earlier he rephrased a saying found in Q in which Jesus declared: "Be merciful as your father is merciful" (Q 6:36; Luke 6:36), so that it reads, "Be perfect as your heavenly father is perfect" (5:48). But for Matthew the meaning is largely the same: perfection is to commit oneself to total obedience to God's will in the spirit of compassion.

Judgment and Compassion

Judgment is a common theme in Matthew and a regular instrument of exhortation. This is not surprising given the close connection Matthew has developed between Jesus and John the Baptist. The Sermon on the Mount ends with the threat of judgment on the bad builders (7:24-27). The major speech in Matthew 13 which uses harvest parables concludes with a similar emphasis on judgment. The final teaching of Jesus' public ministry concludes with parables of judgment on lazy girls, lazy investors, and lazy goats (25:1-48). Where criteria of judgment become explicit, they derive from the Law. Matthew has no hesitation in declaring that the Son of Man will judge all people by their works (16:28). There is no special status, either as children of Abraham or as disciples of Jesus. The same criteria apply. This is totally consistent with John the Baptist's message (3:7-10). Perhaps these criteria come most effectively to expression in that final parable of Jesus' ministry, the parable of the sheep and the goats (25:31-48). Real compassion in real-life situations is what matters. Notice there is nothing about cultic or ritual obligations. It all boils down to compassion.

For Matthew this compassion is for all without discrimination and to be given by all without exception. Yet Matthew now juxtaposes this plea for compassion with a striking lack of compassion; forgiveness is only for a time. The divine institution has been preparing unquenchable fires for all who fail to love and fail to find forgiveness beyond a certain point (25:41). This dichotomy — of love and not love, of compassion and violence, of engagement and abandonment — in the church's first gospel has condemned the church to living out both sides of the coin and bequeathing to the world an ambivalent message of hope and despair, or good and evil, lived out all too often in its own behavior.

Holding Jesus and the Law Together as One

Matthew is the gospel of the scribe. It portrays Jesus in strong continuity with the story of Israel and with Israel's Scripture. Jesus is not an alternative authority to that of Scripture and its Law but an embodiment of it. Yet he is also its supreme interpreter. Matthew portrays Jesus as the coming judge of whom John spoke, who will one day exercise that judgment but who has first come to be Israel's savior by bringing to fulfillment the hopes of the prophets and by expounding the word of the Law. That word of hope, the teaching of God's will, God's Law, focuses not on the words of individual commands so much as on the attitudes and behaviors they imply. In particular, Matthew's approach to the whole of Scripture as promise and command is informed by a theology reflected in Hosea 6:6, which he twice quotes: "I desire mercy and not sacrifice" (9:13; 12:7). For Matthew, as for the prophet, these were not alternatives, but two aspects of the divine order in which the former has greater priority over the latter.

For Matthew, God is merciful and compassionate. God's attitude towards people is to inform the attitudes and behaviors of people towards one another. Matthew retains the tradition of Jesus that people matter most, but much more strongly than Jesus, he has sought to bind this perspective within an approach that saw life in terms of authority, of demand and obedience. This informs the way he develops his thought not only about the Scripture and its tradition, but also about Jesus and about the church.

Matthew's construction is the product of a history in transition. He disapproves of Mark's innovations, based on insights from two decades of living out Christian faith and mission in a Gentile context; but he seems to be about to face the same issues afresh as Gentiles enter his shelter. In a broader sense Matthew has reasserted the essence of Jewish faith: the gift of God's grace — the Law — now borne afresh by

Jesus. Jesus' messiahship poses no conflict with that Law but has evoked rejection from the dominant Jewish groups in Matthew's social context. How can Matthew's church survive being faithful to the Law when living in such isolation? The possible comfort of new Gentile members makes an explosive mix. Even if they also can be persuaded to uphold the Law, there will be the danger that the wider Christian movement, which has become inconsistent in regulating such issues, will call this community into further disrepute and force its hand to new and painful decisions.

Developing the claim to authority has been an important defensive position. It wards off the assertion that Jesus undermines Scripture. It provides a better basis for the community's own claims to authority. It counters the dangerous free-for-all tendencies of Christian groups known to Matthew who have abandoned proper ethical concern and responsibility for each other. It also provides an instrument of control and a way of redefining the gospel as the good news that the Law's demand is not the legalistic application of prescriptions but good instruction informed by care and compassion. It is demanding, but the issue is an attitude to life expressed in behavior. This is a narrow way, but one that can be followed and will lead to life.

The demand structure also makes it possible to lay out a clear set of criteria that will apply at the judgment and thus to employ these rhetorically as a means of persuasion. This reveals some ambiguity in the system. The authority structure that demands love threatens anger and punishment if the demands are not fulfilled. Matthew's theology is in process. Its insights into love have the potential to call into question the structures Matthew favors in supporting it. But this does not happen. There is unfinished business. Part of that is a legacy of hate against Jews and dissenters, as Matthew's structure has been applied to life; both good news and bad news.

Matthew's is the most thoroughgoing of all the gospels in its attempt to hold it all together. Without doubt this reflects a commitment to the religious heritage of Israel and a very high regard for Scripture. The message of Jesus is accommodated within a system designed to ensure unity of authority and coherence. Mark is too radical for

Matthew. Yet Matthew is not a literalist, not a fundamentalist, though of all the gospel writers he is closest to it. Matthew's has been, in many respects, the most influential of all the gospels in shaping the church's life, though not as influential as John's in shaping its thought. But it is a structure that cannot be sustained; it will face a crisis. It now stands in a canon of Scripture where there are solutions to its unfinished issues, including some that its author rejects. Yet it has also provided a grounding of Christian faith in attitude and action that has been a bulwark against ethereal spiritualities and distractions and the naive hopes of those who believe that ethics are somehow automatic or, at best, secondary.

• 5 •

LUKE

Radical Commitment
to People in Need and to Israel

We traditionally attribute two writings of the New Testament to Luke: the Gospel of Luke and the Book of the Acts of the Apostles. They form a two-volume work, now separated from each other in the New Testament by the Gospel of John. Each is formally addressed to a certain Theophilus, probably a patron. This was a common literary custom in writing works of literature for the public market. Luke writes therefore as a historian of his time. This is apparent not only in the formal reference to a patron, but also in the somewhat lavish and complicated sentence with which the work begins. It is, of course, more evident in the original Greek. Here is how it sounds in literal translation:

"Since many have attempted to put together an orderly account of the events which have been fulfilled among us, just as people who were eyewitnesses from the beginning and stewards of the message have passed them on to us, it also seemed right to me, since I have investigated everything closely from the start, to write for you an accurate and orderly account, most excellent Theophilus, so that you may know of the reliability of the matters about which you have been instructed" (Luke 1:1-4).

What a mouthful! Yet it was considered good style to begin one's work with such an impressive, we might say, convoluted sentence.

96

Luke is placing himself in the world of the best writers of the time and reflects the current literary fashion of the Hellenistic Roman world. It is then all the more striking that he immediately turns to a very different style in the verses that follow: "And it came to pass in the days of Herod the king of Judea." In short sentences punctuated with such expressions as "it came to pass" and "and behold" and many *and*s, Luke proceeds to tell the story of the conception, birth, and circumcision of first, John the Baptist and then Jesus. This is no longer the high style of Hellenistic rhetoric, but the narrative style of the Old Testament. Luke can work in both worlds.

Jesus and His Family Keep God's Law

What we observe in style also matches Luke's stance overall. He is a man of his Gentile world, but can move readily and sympathetically in the culture of Judaism. This is an important starting point for considering the way he relates Jesus to the Scriptures and the Law. Luke has no hesitation in portraying Jesus as a Jew who observed the Law and shared the aspirations of his people. This is particularly apparent in the first two chapters, which in some sense set the tone for all that follows.

Zechariah is a priest of the temple. He and Elizabeth were devout. Luke puts it this way: "They were both righteous before God, following all the commandments and ordinances of the Lord blamelessly" (1:6). Luke is not being quaint or antiquarian. He strongly approves of Zechariah and Elizabeth. Nothing suggests he sees them as belonging to a piety of the past; such piety is to remain. The Lord's commands and ordinances set out in Scripture remain forever. We notice the same level of piety in Jesus' family. In 2:21-24 we read that Mary and Joseph had Jesus circumcised on the eighth day. Mary waited until the end of her time of being unclean after giving birth, before going up to the temple to make the offerings prescribed in the Scripture. Luke underlines this strict observance of the Law in 12:8 by citing portions of Exodus (13:2, 12, 15) and Leviticus (5:11) and referring back twice more to this blameless behavior on the part of the holy family (2:27 and again in 2:39).

At this point we strike an oddity. For all Luke's enthusiasm in portraying such observance, by all accounts his description does not reflect accurate knowledge of the practices. Luke speaks of *their* purification, whereas the purification was required only of Mary who bore the child. Similarly, there is no requirement that a woman go to the temple for the purification; that is required only for the offering of the first fruits. It is also a little strange that Luke omits mention of payment of the five shekels to redeem the child (cf. Num. 18:15-16). These are signs that Luke has secondhand knowledge of Jewish practices.

But this does not take away from the fact that Luke affirms careful observance of the Law and emphasizes that in this respect Jesus and his extended family fulfilled all that God required with great care. I have mentioned already that nothing indicates that Luke saw this as a piety which should now be defunct. The commitment to God's Law as set out in Scripture remains a feature of Luke's portrait of Jesus. It comes through in his visit as a twelve-year-old to the temple. Luke emphasizes Jesus' regular attendance at the synagogue. Invitations to dine from leading Pharisees assume Jesus was seen by them as observant. Luke underlines that Jesus prayed regularly, frequently adding it into anecdotes where it had previously gone unmentioned. His commitment to God's temple remains constant throughout, a feature to which we shall return when we discuss Jesus' stance in greater detail.

The Church in Acts Keeps God's Law

Acts, too, commences with a picture of the disciples centered on the temple (2:46). There they worship, and they pray at the hours of sacrifice (3:1; 10:9). Like Zechariah and Elizabeth, Mary and Joseph, Anna and Simeon, they are exemplary and devout. Nothing of their new faith calls their commitment to Scripture and its Law into question. In fact, they, rather than their unbelieving compatriots, are faithful Israel. Nor should the careful observance of the first disciples be seen as a temporary phenomenon. Many have interpreted the results of Peter's vision (10:9-16), the conversion of Cornelius (10:17-48), and the so-called apostolic council of Acts 15 as indicating that these effected a major departure from biblical law, but, as we shall see in more detail later, this is far from the case. In fact, near the end of Acts it becomes quite clear that in Luke's view Christian Jews should be continuing to observe the commandments given them in Scripture.

This comes through most clearly in the case of the apostle Paul. On arrival for the last time in Jerusalem Paul met with James and a delegation of elders from the Jerusalem church (21:18-26). Their major concern was the rumor that Paul had encouraged Christian Jews to abandon the Law, to give up the requirement of circumcision and the like. Luke has them speak of "apostasy from Moses" (21:21). Their concern is not that Paul had in fact taught such things, but that the false rumors should be scotched. Paul obliges by demonstrating his continuing full observance of Scripture by joining publicly with four men who had taken an oath and undergoing with them the required rites of purification and paying for the shaving of their heads. It is, in fact, another instance where Luke appears not to be accurately informed about current practices, but the main point is clear. According to Luke, no one should imagine that Paul gave up observance of what the Law commanded. No one should imagine that a Christian Jew should do anything other than be as pious and observant as had been all the faithful Jews from Zechariah to Jesus, from the first apostles to Paul. The only exception appears to be the requirement of circumcision with regard to non-Jews, but it was more of an exception that proved the rule and certainly not one that applied to Christian Jews.

Two things are striking about Luke's approach. One is the consistency with which he portrays the demand that Scripture and its Law continue to be kept. The other is that in making this point Luke, more often than not, even has in mind ritual and cultic law, such as purification rites, circumcision, temple worship, required offerings, oaths, and the like. He is not just thinking of ethical commands.

According to the Scriptures

Luke also emphasizes fulfillment of Scripture in other ways. On occasions, as we have seen, he even writes in the language and style of the Greek Bible. This was a way of linking the story he tells with the story it tells. Like both Mark and Matthew he also employs the techniques of building echoes of the old stories into the new stories. Luke does this in a very creative way. Elizabeth's plight, that she cannot have children, echoes the plight of Hannah, the mother of Samuel (Luke 1:5-25; 1 Sam. 1). The day of Pentecost is a tapestry of symbolic allusions (Acts 2): the mighty rushing wind, for example. In both Hebrew and Greek the word for wind is the same as the word for spirit. The flames of fire echo the legends about the flame of fire at Sinai which divided into seventy parts representing the seventy nations who then heard and understood the divine law, but only Israel responded.

On many other occasions Luke embedded such allusions into his stories. Even the timeline of early church events, a timeline only Luke employs, reveals his concern to evoke connections, especially through the use of numbers (Acts 1-2). The risen Jesus appears for forty days, a biblical figure with many allusions. The Spirit comes on the fiftieth day (Pentecost means fiftieth), the feast of the harvest, the beginning of the church's mission. The disciples gathered in the upper room numbered one hundred and twenty; ten times twelve. Israel is multiplying. Numbers meant something.

Luke was keen to emphasize Scripture fulfillment. Like the others, he includes reference to the Scriptures which he now sees fulfilled, but he lacks the set formulae of Matthew and his more scribal approach. Luke operates more loosely. Sometimes, as in the conversation between Jesus and the disciples on the Emmaus road, the focus is on the fact of fulfillment of Scripture rather than on any particular Scripture passage (24:25-27, 32).

Luke's Jesus stands firmly within the people of Israel, observes the Law, and expects his own to do the same. He fulfills Scripture both at the level of prediction and at the level of all that he says and does. There is a scripturalness about Luke's account, which reaches from language and style to symbolic and sometimes literal allusion to the Old Testament. Overlaying this are also regular signs of divine involvement. Dreams, visions, angelic appearances — all enhance the sense that what we have here is divine history, fully in accord with God's action in the past.

Sharing Jewish Hopes

The Jewishness, that is, the commitment to continuity with Israel and with Scripture, also comes to expression in the way that Luke identifies with Jewish aspirations. The angelic announcements, the song of Mary (1:46-55), the blessing of Zechariah (1:67-79), and the oracle of Simeon (2:29-32) in the first two chapters relate directly to Jesus and John. But they also give expression to Israel's hopes. The references to Jesus and John do not exhaust the relevance of these expressions of hope. The hope that the mighty will be cast down from their thrones and the humble lifted up, that Israel will be delivered from her enemies, that the Messiah will reign in peace, is not to be reduced to rhetorical flourish. The disciples on the Emmaus road, who like Zechariah and Anna had hoped for the liberation of Israel (24:21), were not deluded about the kingdom of God. When the disciples asked the risen Lord whether he would at that time restore the kingdom to Israel (Acts 1:6), it was not a silly question. Jesus does not scold them for getting the agenda wrong; he only tells them not to focus on the timing (1:7). There are things that have to happen in the meantime. There is work to do: be witnesses to the ends of the earth (1:8).

In Luke, Jesus foretells the sacking of their city and destruction of the temple (19:41-44; 23:27-31). More than any other gospel Luke portrays Jesus' grief at the suffering that awaits Jerusalem. It will be surrounded and brought low. But then, Luke tells us, the time of trampling by the Gentiles will give way to the return of Jesus, whom the citizens of Jerusalem will hail (Luke 21:20-28; 13:34-35). With him comes the liberation for which Israel has longed. Now the kingdom will be restored to Israel. Jesus and his twelve will rule over Israel in justice and peace

(22:28-30). Jerusalem will be restored as the holy city, the city from which it all began and to which Paul so constantly returned. Luke 21:32 expresses the hope that this will become reality within a generation.

There is, therefore, in Luke's writings a very favorable stance towards Jewishness. That means a very committed stance towards Scripture and its commands for Israel. Even if Luke holds this conviction at a distance and sometimes errs in detail, there can be no question of his commitment to Scripture in this respect and to Israel's hopes. Unlike Matthew, who affirms biblical law but focuses almost entirely on ethics, Luke's emphasis is all inclusive. He encompasses the whole Law as the focus of attention, ethical and ritual, and more than that, affirms the specific hopes of Israel for its liberation. It is in this context that we approach his portrait of Jesus and his ministry, for it enables us to make sense of the way Luke tells the story.

Jesus and John and the Law

It is not possible in the scope of this chapter to follow that story in detail or even in overview, let alone its extension into the Acts of the Apostles. Instead I want to review briefly the opening scenes and then draw together major trends which, I believe, are present throughout.

We saw that Matthew makes much of the figure of John the Baptist, and this significantly affected also his portrait of Jesus. In Luke the situation is quite different even though Luke shares largely the same sources as Matthew. In Matthew John addresses the Pharisees and Sadducees. In Luke John addresses the crowds (3:7-9). Both challenge the false sense of security which some find in being descendants of Abraham. That counts for nothing if there is no fruit. Both emphasize the importance of repentance, baptism, and a commitment to keeping God's Law. In Luke this is even expanded; John addresses the people, the toll collectors and soldiers, about the practical implications of keeping God's Law in terms of avoiding exploitation of the needy and vulnerable (3:10-14). But Luke does not introduce the sense of conflict with Jewish authorities as does Matthew.

Matthew had John proclaim the kingdom of God using the same summary of proclamation he would use later of Jesus and the disciples (Matt. 3:2). His introduction of Jesus as judge to come defined a major aspect of Jesus' role. Luke does not have John proclaim the same message as Jesus. And while Luke includes the predictions of Jesus' role as judge, in comparison with Matthew he has already included much more in his infancy narratives to shape his hearers' expectations about Jesus. The hearers already know that this Jesus comes to bring Israel's hopes of liberation and peace to fulfillment as Israel's Messiah.

These expectations are then recalled when Luke has John explicitly deny that he, himself, was the hoped-for Messiah (3:15). The result, therefore, is quite a different focus in presenting Jesus. Whereas Matthew begins with the image of Jesus the judge, as defined by John, who will illustrate his own total obedience in temptation and go on to defend and expound the Law, Luke's Jesus already has a wider agenda before Luke reports John's words. John's image of Jesus the judge carries less weight. Luke shares the story of Jesus' obedience in the face of temptation, but the Jesus who is baptized and who weathers that storm is the Jesus of the particular hopes of Israel. This focus on Israel is also reflected in the fact that in Luke the temptations come to a climax in Jerusalem at the temple, not on a mountain viewing the kingdoms of the world as in Matthew (4:1-13; cf. Matt. 4:1-11).

Jesus Announces His Agenda

The agenda of Jesus, according to Luke, comes to the fore in the account of Jesus' visit to his hometown synagogue (4:16-30). Jesus stands up and reads from Isaiah 61:1, applying to himself the prophet's words that the spirit had anointed him to bring healing and liberation and to proclaim good news to the poor. There are strong echoes of the vision of salvation of the first chapters. Disaffection sets in as people realize that Jesus is "just the boy from down the road," so to speak, and that he had not done marvels in his hometown as he had in Capernaum. The provincialism of this response seems to function in Luke as an indicator of a greater provincialism to come. When Jesus answers their concern by pointing to the blessing that came through the prophets to the non-Israelites, the widow of Zarephath, and Naaman the Syrian, the locals are offended. At one level the story paints Nazareth as jealous of Capernaum; but at another level Luke is probably foreshadowing the later response of some Jews to the expansion of the mission to Gentiles and the resultant parting of the ways.

In this initial incident we find, therefore, many of the issues at the heart of Luke's portrait of Jesus, and especially of his attitude towards Scripture. The first is Luke's note that Jesus entered the synagogue on the sabbath day as was his custom. This belongs to Luke's understanding of Jesus as an observant Jew. He will send lepers to the temple to undergo the rites of purification required in biblical law (5:12-16; 17:12-19). He will travel to Jerusalem for the feast of the Passover, as he had as a child. He will show concern about corruption in the temple. This is the praying Jesus, the Jesus who stands fast in temptation. Going to the synagogue on the sabbath was a natural part of sabbath observance of the time.

Similarly, the reading from Scripture underlines the important theme in Luke that Jesus and the events of his life fulfill Scripture. The actual contents of the prophetic word also reflect Luke's understanding of Jesus. "The Spirit of the Lord is upon me, because he has anointed me to proclaim good news to the poor. He has sent me to announce freedom to the captives and recovery of sight to the blind, to bring release for the oppressed, to announce the year of God's grace."

Luke has, by this scene, effectively replaced Mark 1:14-15. There we read that Jesus went into Galilee, proclaiming, "The time is fulfilled; the kingdom of God is at hand; repent and believe the gospel." In its place Luke has placed an expanded version of Mark 6:1-6, where Mark described Jesus' rejection in the synagogue at Nazareth. The reading from the prophet is part of the expansion. It still has the message of kingdom summarized in Mark 1:14-15 in mind, but by using the reading from Isaiah 61 Luke has given greater substance to its hope and set up the basis for what Jesus will proclaim in the following chapters.

The next major occasion where Luke's Jesus gives an address is

6:20-49, which begins with the words: "Blessed are you poor, for yours is the kingdom of God; Blessed are you who are hungry, for you shall be satisfied. Blessed are you who weep, for you shall laugh." This is the good news for the poor. Luke is revisiting Jesus' agenda announced at Nazareth of proclaiming good news to the poor. The sentiments also echo those of the songs and hymns of the infancy narratives. The events of liberation that await their future fulfillment are already to become reality in the lives of people during Jesus' ministry. Anecdotes that follow this episode illustrate its promise.

This agenda of the kingdom is also echoed when Luke uses the Q story about John sending his disciples to Jesus. They ask if he is the one announced by John. Jesus responds by pointing to his deeds in language that echoes the prophetic hopes for healing and deliverance. What Jesus announced in Nazareth he now explains has come true in reality. "Go and tell John what you have seen and heard: blind people are recovering their sight; the lame are walking; lepers are cleansed and the deaf hear, the dead are raised, the poor receive good news" (Luke 7:22). In Matthew this passage responds to the disparity sensed between the role John announced for the coming one and Jesus' actions. In Luke such disparity is not acute. Rather the passage reinforces the focus of Jesus' message: he announces good news to the poor; the poor are blessed because theirs is the hope of the kingdom of God.

This is an important statement because it sets the focus. It tells us about the kingdom of God, about God's reign and God's agenda. It therefore also tells us about Luke's approach to Scripture, or at least, the way Luke portrays Jesus' approach to Scripture and the Law in particular. After this rejection at Nazareth, Luke initially avoids portraying Jesus as in conflict with the religious authorities. He even omits Mark's contrast between Jesus' authority and that of the scribes and between his new teaching and theirs (4:31-37; cf. Mark 1:21-28). Jesus' authority stands alone. Initially Luke is celebrating the breaking in of God's kingdom through Jesus' ministry. Conflicts are distractions and will come later.

The events of liberation are drawn from stories in Mark. They included also the healing of Peter's mother-in-law, of many people gathered on the evening after the sabbath, the enlisting of disciples, and the healing of a leper (4:38–5:16; cf. Mark 1:16-45). Jesus sent the leper off to the temple in accordance with the prescriptions of the Law. Many more such miracles will follow. The evidence of what Jesus told John's disciples to report to their master, the signs of the kingdom, the fulfillment of the agenda, will be amply displayed. The values of the kingdom, lived out already in Jesus' ministry, are Luke's primary focus when it comes to interpreting Scripture and scriptural law. Often, however, these values emerge in the context of conflict.

Conflict over Interpreting the Law

The tension foreshadowed in the way the congregation at Nazareth responded to Jesus (4:16-30) soon finds its echo in Luke's story of Jesus' ministry. And when finally Luke moves to the material he found in Mark directly related to conflict, he takes the first — the occasion of the healing of the paralytic let down through the roof — and makes it into a confrontation on a grander scale (6:17-26; cf. Mark 2:1-12). He adds two things: Jesus was already exhibiting God's power in healing when this event occurred; and teachers of the Law had gathered on the occasion from all over Galilee. One has the impression of a major showdown. In it Luke exposes their accusation of blasphemy as patently false; Jesus was not claiming to forgive sins independently of God. His powerful healing activity was obvious proof that God was on his side.

Luke will have been aware that the religious authorities had similar misgivings about the somewhat innovative activities of John the Baptist in offering forgiveness of sins (cf. 20:1-8). It was hard to fit such unorthodox approaches into the established pattern according to which the primary mediation of forgiveness came through the temple. But there was nothing contrary to biblical law in either John's actions or Jesus' declaration.

In retelling the call of Levi and the account of the banquet where Jesus is present with toll collectors and sinners, Luke has merged the two so that Levi now hosts it (6:27-35). Again Jesus rejects the implied allegations that he contravened the Law. It would have been hard to make such a charge stick. Keeping the company of evil people is certainly frowned upon in Scripture, but there are no absolutes. Keeping the company of people who may well have neglected tithing laws and purity laws about preparation of food came under the same censure generally, but it was similarly hard to substantiate the charge that this was directly against scriptural law. Jesus' defense here as elsewhere was concern for these people.

Luke offers a number of other instances where the issue comes forward. He knows the Q tradition where Jesus confronted the crowds for being like children in the marketplace fighting over noncooperation (7:31-35). The accusations Jesus cites against himself are that he is a glutton and drunkard because he keeps such company. Luke has Jesus defend his stance against such accusations with the parables of the lost sheep, the lost coin, and the prodigal son (15:1-32). For Luke, Jesus' mixing with such people is a strategy of love. It is a way of calling sinners to repentance. Luke was probably not comfortable with Jesus' simply being there without such an evangelistic strategy in mind. But underlying his view is that such love is to be the highest priority in determining God's will. The ground has shifted slightly from what was probably not simply a strategy for evangelism on the part of Jesus, but partly an expression of celebration and acceptance. Nevertheless Luke retains compassion as the center of Jesus' response in such matters. Fundamentally God is compassionate, and God's Law should be read accordingly. The issues of mixing with toll collectors and sinners will become relevant also when we discuss its more radical extension, namely, the inclusion of Gentiles. We return to this below.

This principle that compassion matters most comes through also in the four occasions that Luke reports as conflict over sabbath law. In the first, in defense of the disciples' plucking grain on the sabbath, Jesus asserts his own authority over the sabbath as Son of Man, a designation strongly linked with authority (6:1-5). The three other incidents show that this did not mean, for Luke, the authority to waive the sabbath law, but rather the authority to interpret it (6:6-11; 13:10-17;

14:1-6). This authority was from God, and Luke makes it clear that it is God's priorities which should determine sabbath law interpretation. Here again, compassion for the needy prevails. It is right to heal the man with the withered hand on the sabbath, to heal the woman crippled for eighteen years, to heal the man who had dropsy. There is also an undercurrent of popular common sense appeal operating in these stories in the spirit of "Let's be reasonable; to withhold healing just because it is the sabbath is absurd." But Luke will not have seen this as acting contrary to the biblical sabbath law.

From Luke one has the impression that criticism from the teachers of the Law is an annoying distraction to be dealt with on the side. Thus Luke sees no need, as does Matthew, to be on the defensive about Jesus and the Law. This is most evident in the contrast between the sermon in 6:20-39, drawn largely from Q, and the greatly expanded version we know as the Sermon on the Mount in Matthew. As we have shown, there the issue of the Law is of paramount concern. Jesus makes basic statements of principle to counter misapprehensions and accusations: "Do not think that I have come to annul the Law and the Prophets; I have not come to annul, but to fulfill them." In Luke's shorter version of the sermon there is nothing of the kind. Jesus' teaching in Luke's sermon is also ultimately an exposition of the Law; Leviticus 19:18 ("You shall love your neighbor as yourself") lies not far below the surface. But Luke sees no need to demonstrate the sermon's coherence with Scripture. Luke's concern is not scribal like Matthew's.

The Law and Compassion for the Poor

It is the God whose agenda is concern for the poor who informs the biblical interpretation of Luke's Jesus. This comes particularly to the fore where the issue of the status of the biblical law is addressed directly. Luke 16:16-17 preserves a major statement from Q about the status of the Law and the Prophets. They read, "The Law and the Prophets were until John; since then the kingdom of God is proclaimed and everyone is forcing their way into it. But it is easier for heaven and earth to pass away than for one stroke of the Law to fall." This is not like a relay race where the baton is passed to the kingdom of God and the Law and Prophets cease to be in force. On the contrary, the saying in 16:18 — which applies a strict law about divorce — shows that the contrary is the case. The coming of the kingdom reinforces what the Law demands. It remains totally valid, just as also John's teaching remains valid.

The statement, "And all are forcing their way into it," is enigmatic. It could mean, they are trying to do so or that their action in some way is in conflict with the kingdom. Luke 16:17 certainly counters the implication that may derive from their action or attempted action, namely that the Law's demands are to be diminished. In the wider context of this passage in chapter 16 Luke has brought material together dealing with wealth. Even the forbidding of divorce should probably be seen in this context, namely divorce for greed, to gain a richer dowry. Certainly the preceding verses contrast serving God and serving mammon (16:13-15), and the parable with which the chapter begins now serves to address abuse of wealth (16:1-12). The same is true of the parable with which the chapter ends: the rich man and Lazarus (16:19-31). The message, directed in part at the Pharisees, applies to all, and doubtless to many in Luke's community. It is unambiguous: being in the kingdom means keeping God's Law, and that applies especially to the way we use wealth. That had already been the focus in John's instruction to the crowds, the toll collectors, and the soldiers (3:10-14). It belongs also to the agenda of the kingdom which is meant to be good news for the poor — in real terms, not just in some spiritual sense (4:18; 6:20; 7:22).

The final verses of the parable have Abraham placing side by side the message of the Law and the Prophets and the message, by implication, of the risen Jesus. He says: "If they do not listen to Moses and the Prophets, neither will they obey if someone should rise from the dead" (16:31). Luke assumes absolute coherence between both. Jesus and the Law and the Prophets are one; there are not two different messages.

The same understanding of the single message of both Jesus and the Scriptures comes to expression also in Luke's version of Mark's anecdote in which a scribe asks Jesus which is the greatest commandment (cf. Mark 12:28-34). Luke has trimmed and rewritten the episode and includes it in 10:25-37, with an expanded answer. He has also changed the nature of the question from what it was in Mark. In Mark it was about which was the greatest commandment. In Luke's version it is now the same as the one brought by the rich ruler in 18:18-23, which is based on Mark 10:17-22. That question is: "What must I do to inherit eternal life?"

The answer Jesus gives in Luke 10 is to point to the Law and ask what it says. When the man cites the command to love God and love one's neighbor, Jesus agrees. "Do this and you will live." Luke's Jesus does not believe that the man's answer was wrong. You gain eternal life by keeping the Law. On the other hand, Luke would not have understood this as implying that only the Law mattered, that Jesus was unimportant. On the contrary, for Luke they were one. The Law, like Jesus, declared God's will. Doing God's will as set out in the Law and by Jesus is the way to salvation. There was no sense that the man had to choose between loyalty to Jesus and loyalty to the Law. For Luke they are one and the same.

The man's attempt at self-justification then evokes a parable from the lips of Jesus, the famous parable of the Good Samaritan. In an interesting twist the Samaritan who helps out a desperate victim portrays the neighbor; for Jesus asks the man, Who in the story proved to be neighbor to the person in need? We mostly think of the desperate victim as the neighbor. By turning these expectations upside down the parable confronts the man with a person who often faced discrimination on religious grounds: a Samaritan. It is not just that the neighbor is human; he is also potentially caring, a bearer of divine compassion. The story cleverly contrasts such love with the preoccupation of the religious who passed the desperate man by. Luke is not attacking the institution of priesthood, Levites, or the temple, but a perverted orientation. But he is making it very clear: keeping the Law in this spirit is the way of salvation. So Jesus says to the man: "Go and do likewise."

The same focus on compassion for the poor is evident in Luke's

version of the rich man's encounter with Jesus, already mentioned
(18:18-23; cf. Mark 10:17-22). By making him a ruler Luke underlines
his wealth. The same question is asked: "What must I do to inherit
eternal life?" Jesus gives a similar answer. Keep the commandments.
The challenge that the man sell what he has and give to the poor and
follow Jesus should not be understood as stage two of the conditions
for salvation, but as Jesus' subtle exposure of what was wrong with the
man. Keeping the commandments means nothing if there is not a
commitment to compassion for the poor. Asking this particular man
to sell his goods exposed this failure.

We see then that for Luke upholding the Law is not preliminary or
peripheral, but essential for salvation; Jesus declared this to be so, so
that to follow Jesus means to take this seriously. The Christian life
means acknowledging who Jesus is and heeding his instruction; right
at the heart of his instruction is the demand that we obey God's Law as
set forth in the Scriptures and do so in the spirit of Jesus. The orientation towards love and compassion for the needy was not a novel approach. Matthew illustrates its roots in the prophets. It has its foundation in Jesus' own teaching and permeates the tradition of the
teachings of Jesus. It also had its contemporary appeal in Luke's cul-
tured world. Friendship, practical caring, and sharing of possessions
had become significant virtues to be praised and sought after. They
represented key themes of the popular philosophers of the day, so that
Luke's portrait of Jesus would find a positive echo. Interpreting Scripture never takes place in a vacuum with regard to values. Just as in
Mark they shaped his critical stance towards cult and rite, so in Luke
they reinforce the appeal of compassion and care for the poor.

Indeed, Luke steps right into one of the beloved institutions of the
day, the banquet, when he has Jesus declare that people should give
preference to inviting the poor and the outcast and the lame (14:16-
24). There is a sense in which it is this same compassion for the poor
that draws together these stories of example and exhortation and those
where Luke shows Jesus defending his own actions. The difference is
that in the latter, compassion is not only for the worthy — namely the
poor, the needy, the underdog — but also for the sinners, the crimi-

nals, the rogues. The latter stance sits less comfortably with the prevailing values of the time, Luke's and ours.

Confronting Religious Authorities

The confrontation of the religious in the parable of the Good Samaritan echoes the stance taken in the attack on the scribes and the Pharisees. Using Q material Luke repeats the accusations of Jesus that these Pharisees are too concerned with purification of a vessel's exterior while the inside was full of greed and wickedness, perhaps even quite literally filled with the fruits of such action (11:37-41). This is not an attack on purification as such but on the failure to attend to ethical issues. The conclusion that all things would be clean for them if they attended rightly to justice for the poor should also not be seen as a shortcut past purification laws.

It is similar with tithes, where according to Luke, Jesus attacks attention to the tithing of such things as herbs while neglecting justice and the love of God (11:42). The attack is not on tithing laws but on failure in what matters more. It is similar with attacks on self-seeking and hypocrisy (11:43). Luke also has Jesus address criticism to the scribes, those more directly responsible for interpreting Scripture, for the burdens their rulings impose on people and for their unwillingness to offer relief to those bearing such burdens (11:46). In each case it is abuse that is under fire, never the Scripture and its laws. This coheres with the fact that otherwise Luke shows unerring positive regard for ritual and cultic provisions of the Law.

About Gentiles and Omitting Mark's Solution

The episode in the synagogue at Nazareth foreshadows, as we have already intimated, a more contentious problem, the inclusion of Gentiles. To some extent Jesus' defense against the accusation that he dines with toll collectors and sinners might equally apply to inclusion of Gentiles. To that degree the elder brother in the story of the prodigal son matches the response of the Nazareth congregation when Jesus mentions that God blessed Gentiles through the prophets; but the analogy is not exact. Including sinners of Israel who are children of Abraham is one thing. Including Gentiles is another. Luke goes out of his way to emphasize the inclusiveness of Jesus; he includes women, he includes the poor, the outcast, the sinners who repent. With Zacchaeus's repentance Jesus declares that salvation had come to his house, but notice why: because he, too, is a son of Abraham (19:9). Going to the house of a Gentile is quite another matter.

We see this in the way Luke carefully rewrites the story of Jesus and the centurion with the sick slave (7:1-10; cf. Matt. 8:5-13; John 4:46-54). In Luke's version the centurion does not even meet Jesus. Acknowledging the problem of having Jesus come under his roof, the centurion's words — preserved in almost identical form in Matthew and Luke — are now passed on to Jesus secondhand. Luke keeps Jesus not only away from the house, but away from the Gentile as well. And there is more: in order to justify Jesus' positive response, Luke gives an account of the impeccable character of the centurion, in particular, his generosity towards the local Jewish community. In the same way he will justify the centurion Cornelius in Acts as being a Jew in almost every other respect, an exemplary Godfearer (Acts 10:1-2, 35). Luke is highly sensitive to the issues and even assumes a rather conservative stance on Jewish law.

The story of the two centurions match each other. In both, the issue is entry into a Gentile's house. In the first story there is no contact; Jesus heals the slave at distance. In the story in Acts, Peter ventures across the boundary, but only after extraordinary divine intervention to legitimate his act. We shall return to that shortly. Within the gospel we find hints of inclusion of Gentiles, but we find no indication that this is to be achieved by any modification of the Law.

At this point we must consider Luke's handling of Mark's special composition in Mark 6–7. We recall that Mark employs the feeding of the five thousand and four thousand as symbols for the word of God coming to both Israel and the Gentiles, and he has composed the section around a disputation about hand washing. In Mark's composition the dispute becomes the occasion for Jesus to declare concern with food laws and outward purity of no significance, thus to negate large parts of the Law. In doing so, he removed what had been a major obstacle to ongoing relations between Jews and Gentiles, at least from the perspective of fairly conservative Jews. That was Mark's extrapolation of where he saw Jesus' teaching to be leading. We saw that Matthew disagreed and therefore radically reworked the composition to remove the celebration of Gentile inclusion. In Matthew Jesus rejects only an extremist demand for ritual washing of hands before meals, nothing more. Both feedings now celebrate God's word in Jesus to Israel.

Luke is equally resolute. He retains the sequence of events recorded in Mark, beginning with the sending out of the twelve disciples (9:1-6; cf. Mark 6:7-13). There follows, as in Mark, a reference to John the Baptist's death at the hands of Herod, but severely abbreviated (9:7-9; cf. Mark 6:14-31). Luke then has Jesus take the disciples to Bethsaida, where Jesus feeds the five thousand (9:10-17; cf. Mark 6:32-44). Luke's story then jumps across nearly two chapters of Mark, from Mark 6:45 to 8:26. These chapters make up the bulk of Mark's careful composition celebrating Gentile inclusion and rejecting food laws. The most likely explanation is that Luke, like Matthew, found Mark's radicalism unacceptable, but instead of reworking the material, simply omitted it. There are indications that this is what happened. Mark does not place the feeding of the five thousand at Bethsaida, but at the end of the section that Luke has omitted, that is where they are. Jesus healed the blind man at Bethsaida (Mark 8:22-26). So Luke places the feeding in Bethsaida and makes it easier to pick up the thread of Mark's story immediately after the healing at Bethsaida.

This means that Luke spares the hearer any suggestion that the Law, even a stroke of it, let alone whole sections of it, are set aside, as in Mark. Out also goes the story of the Syrophoenician woman who persuades Jesus to cross the boundary. The offending sections disappear. This is not to say they do not find an echo elsewhere in Luke. We have already noted that in introducing the woes, Luke speaks of Jesus' being confronted for not washing before a meal. That has some similarity with the hand-washing controversy in Mark 7. The conclusion about all things being clean if attention is given to ethical purity may also be a faint echo of Mark 7, but nothing in the gospel indicates that Luke agreed with the stance Mark espoused.

About the Temple: Disagreeing with Mark

In the same way, Luke removes the disparaging treatment of the temple by Mark, who sandwiches the account of Jesus' action in the temple within the story of the cursed and then shriveled fig tree and suggests that the church is the new temple (19:41-48; cf. Mark 11:12-25). The trial no longer has allegations that Jesus would destroy the temple, and so Mark's statement that it was a temple built with hands to be replaced by a temple not built with hands has disappeared (cf. Mark 14:58). Luke will make use of this material in Acts, but not in the way Mark meant it. Mark's symbolic allusions to Christ as the foundation of a new temple, the new temple community of prayer, have gone. By contrast, for Luke, Jesus' concerns are for reform of the existing temple and grief at its coming destruction.

It is at this point that we must look across to Acts. This is relevant not only for the way Luke understands the temple and its place, but also for the contentious issue of the inclusion of Gentiles. Some indeed have found it hard to relate the approach in Acts to the approach in the gospel, suggesting that Luke espoused total faithfulness to the Bible and its Law for the period of Jesus and then applied either erratically or intentionally another standard for the period of the church. Both views represent to my mind an incorrect assessment of the evidence.

The first great controversy surrounds Stephen. It comes after Luke has reported the faithful gatherings of the disciples in the temple. The first Christians were temple centered, were obviously at home there, and followed all the required procedures of temple worship; Luke reports nothing to the contrary. It then comes as quite a surprise that

Greek-speaking Jews raise allegations against Stephen that he had spoken against the Law, Moses, and the temple, and had predicted that Jesus would destroy the temple (Acts 6:8-15). In composing this section of his history, Luke is reusing material he had dropped from the account of Jesus' trial in Mark. Luke reports that these allegations are false, which is what the narrative would lead one to suspect. Stephen then stands trial before the Sanhedrin and in a speech that surveys the sweep of Israel's early history declares God's judgment (Acts 7).

The speech, following prophetic tradition, accosts Israel for its unbelief. Within the course of it Stephen mentions the tent of meeting given to Israel in the wilderness, the settlement in the land, David's request that he be allowed to build a temple, and Solomon's action of building it. At this point the speech declares that God does not dwell in temples made with hands, quoting Isaiah 66:1 to the effect that heaven is God's throne and earth his footstool, so that no one can build a home or resting place for God (7:48-50). This is all very orthodox; Solomon prayed in similar terms at the dedication of the temple (1 Kings 8:27).

Stephen concludes by attacking the Jewish leaders for the stiff-necked resistance to God's word and their uncircumcised hearts (7:51-53). His attack is not on the temple itself, but on its leaders for their refusal to respond to God's Spirit and their persecution and murder of God's messengers. The speech ends with these words: "You received the Law by the hands of angels, but you have not kept it" (7:53). The primary focus was rejection of Jesus, but it also included rejection of the warnings given by the prophets and most recently by Jesus about corruption and abuse of the temple system. It was in response to the charge that they failed to keep the Law, a constant theme in the gospel, that they responded in violence, as a result of which Stephen became the first martyr.

Luke, as we have noted, has employed motifs drawn from Mark's account of Jesus' trial. As well as the false allegations that Jesus would destroy the temple, we also find the reference to the temple as "made with hands," and Stephen's last words about the Son of Man at God's right hand (cf. Mark 14:56-59, 62). As well as this, we find an echo of

Jesus' prayer for forgiveness for his killers, from Luke's crucifixion scene (23:34). But in doing so Luke has not taken over Mark's negative attitude to the temple itself, which reduced its function to a place of prayer and saw it replaced by the community of faith. For Luke the temple functioned and would continue to function as a center of the Jerusalem Christian community and a place to which the faithful like Paul would return.

Gentiles and the Law in Acts

The second set of incidents in Acts which appear related to Mark's approach are those connected with Cornelius, the centurion. When Peter sees a vision, refuses the command to eat unclean animals and is reprimanded for calling what God had made unclean (10:9-16), one might expect that the message was that of Mark 7, which Luke had failed to include: all foods had been declared clean. I find it hard to believe that the vision would not have had such a meaning at some stage. Yet in Acts Luke draws no such implication; where one might expect it, as in the discussion of food laws in Acts 15, it is completely ignored. Instead, the vision now functions only at a symbolic level. Its application is not to foods but to people (10:17-33). Cornelius is not unclean. Peter should not recoil from meeting him. Peter declares that this was a change from what he believed was lawful, but it is not clear that Luke will have seen this as a breach of biblical law (10:28). Peter's visit results in the conversion of a Gentile who receives the Spirit (10:34-48). This event confirms for Peter (and for Luke) the legitimacy of Peter's preaching the gospel to Gentiles (11:1-18; 15:6-9). Luke notes that it happened elsewhere as well, as Greek-speaking Christian Jews were forced to flee Jerusalem and shared their new faith in the synagogues (11:19-27).

Luke tells us that the new movement increasingly attracted Gentiles and that in many situations circumcision was not imposed. This provoked a crisis in the church. The Bible unambiguously demands that Gentiles who wish to join God's people be circumcised.

This was the instruction given to Abraham and recorded in Genesis 17. There can be no tampering with God's word. All the standard arguments would have been there to defend the established position; after all, who are human beings to pick and choose between God's commands!

Yet a compromise was reached at the so-called council of Jerusalem (15:1-29). God's blessing of Gentiles with the Spirit was seen as sufficient warrant to waive the command with regard to Gentiles. Within the world of possibilities present in Luke's narrative, one might have contemplated someone espousing the view that Peter's vision also waived food laws, indeed, waived them for Jews as well as Gentiles, but that is not what occurred. There are comments that might appear to be heading in this direction. Paul declares that in Jesus forgiveness is possible from all that the Law of Moses could not forgive (13:38-39). This may be Luke's attempt to represent a distant memory of Paul's actual stance, but it is garbled. There were no sins for which there was no forgiveness, so that at most we might envisage that the difference was accessibility to the means of forgiveness. In John and Jesus this was made less formal. It is hard to build too much on Luke's portrait of Paul, whom he otherwise represents as totally Law observant. The other person who could be read as promoting a more liberal stance is Peter, who in Acts 15:10-11 may be heard disparaging the Law as burdensome and therefore not to be imposed on Gentiles. It appears however that this should not be seen as an attack on the Law, but rather as a confession of weakness on the part of Jews.

In fact the solution of the Jerusalem conference makes no changes for Jews. For Gentiles it exempts them from circumcision and apart from that imposes on them what has sometimes been called the apostolic decree, which Luke espouses (15:29). It requires Gentile converts to observe certain laws concerning food — in particular, modes of slaughtering meat — and concerning sexual morality. Luke appears to assume that this is what in effect the Law demands of Gentiles, so that, with the exception of circumcision, from which there was a special dispensation by divine intervention, now all Jews and Gentiles abide by what the biblical law requires.

Luke's Solution

For Luke, then, there is absolutely no ground for any accusation on the part of Jews that the Christian church has compromised the Scriptures in its expansion. Luke, therefore, frames the conflict between Christians and Judaism as he does in the incident at Nazareth. It is simply a form of narrow provincialism without foundation, an irrational resentment of the Gentiles' receiving blessing. In relation to the claims of Judaism he asserts that its leaders are misguided in their emphasis on externals and neglect of the heart of the Scripture. To force Christianity back into the old Judaic mold would be to rend the new cloth and waste the new wine.

Luke consistently maintains an attitude of total compliance towards the Bible and its Law and portrays this as the position of the church. It is a position not without difficulty. Jews then and now would scarcely agree and certainly resent the accusation of provincialism and jealousy. It is also a position hard to maintain about the early church, even on Luke's version of affairs. The material Luke has employed in Acts allows us to see that there were alternative positions which Luke had passed over, or, better, papered over with very thin see-through paper. It appears that the issues were no longer live ones for Luke. This is not because Jewish Christianity had ceased to be. It seems to have been alive and well. As a Gentile Luke identifies with Jewish hopes. Luke narrates fondly the stories of the faithful Jews and with only the occasional inaccuracy portrays their practices sympathetically. He never understood Jesus' attacks on hypocrisy or false priorities as a rejection of biblical law or of Jewishness. He rejected any notion that Jesus changed the Law. The Law remained in force.

Scripture and Culture

Yet it is fascinating that while maintaining such a stance, Luke couches Jewish observance in a cultural perspective. True, God has given this Law to the Jews — this ethical and cultic, ritual law. But Luke frequently describes the latter as "customs" of the Jews, a term also occasionally used by Jewish writers (Philo, Josephus) in a cross-cultural context (Acts 6:14; 15:1; 21:21; 28:17). In other words, they apply only to Jews and should be seen as the particular practices of a people. They are divinely sanctioned law, but not universal. In this way Luke can apparently sit comfortably with having Christian Jews obligated to obey such laws to the full and Gentiles obeying just a selection and focusing on ethical law in particular. He can do this partly because he believes the Spirit brought the church to such insight; partly because the ethical laws had universal appeal, and partly because the other laws could be treated as particular and be recognized as such.

Luke's sensitivity to religion as culture also enables him to entertain God's presence within other cultures, one of the few biblical writers to do so. He depicts Paul citing the Greek poet Aratus with approval when he speaks of people being the offspring of God (Acts 17:28). Luke can entertain the possibility that the Spirit also inspired poets and prophets beyond Palestine.

In this sense Luke is a pioneer of the cultural perspective in handling religious authority. This is different from Mark's approach, which can disparage such particular traditions as irrelevant. With Luke there is far greater tolerance, but a tolerance that implicitly relativizes them. He is quite happy to portray the faithful of Jesus' family, Jesus and the disciples as observing ritual and cultic law. He does so at a distance; he is telling of *their* piety, not his own. This is markedly different from Matthew, who is in the thick of it and claiming the only appropriate interpretation of biblical tradition as a Jew. His scarce attention to cultic and ritual practices reflects that his priorities lie elsewhere, while not rejecting them. In Luke one senses almost a cultural admiration. He can include such detail and even enhance it.

Nevertheless within his inclusiveness he leaves us in no doubt where the heart of scriptural law lies: in compassion for the poor. All of the rest remains valid for the Christian Jew, and a modicum of it for the Gentile, but the crunch issues are: believing that Jesus is the Messiah and obeying God's word in accordance with his exposition. His exposition is not selective within Scripture, but it does put some things more at the center than others. Luke shares this with other traditions about Jesus. Perhaps the distinctive thing about Luke's version is the extent to which he details that compassion in relation to issues of wealth and poverty and related marginalization. It is true that his version of the beatitudes has them directed to the disciples, but elsewhere it is equally clear that compassion for the poor is much more than caring for fellow believers.

Unity

The other feature of Luke's achievement which merits attention is his attempt to show a sense of unity emerging from the conflicts and tensions of the early church. Perhaps his position reflects the dominant one of his day. In rewriting the history this sense of unity is achieved at some cost. There is no way that the Paul of the letters can be made to cohere with Luke's reconstruction. Contrary to Luke, what James and his elders feared about Paul was not false but true; we have it firsthand from Paul's writings. Paul's observance was mostly motivated by strategy, not commitment. He was happy to be a Jew for Jews and a Greek for Greeks. He did not live as a Jew. Paul belongs much more in Mark's camp. But Luke, for whom Paul was a hero, writes at perhaps three or four decades distance when fine distinctions have merged and the compromise of the apostolic decree had won the day.

But even within Luke's account the tensions are just below the surface. One has the sense that Luke has scarcely recognized the extent to which his accounts at times expose the weakness of his reconstruction. Peter's vision doubtless functioned at some stage as an attack on food laws, and Luke's silence about its implications is remarkable, so remarkable that there are many who would argue that Luke really is inconsistent here.

Luke's concern was the strength of the church in unity, but he may have tried too hard. Yet overall he presents a unified stance. The Bible remains one and unified. No stroke of its demands has fallen; the exception of circumcision proves the rule. Jesus preaches the Bible's message. Keeping the Law is the way to eternal life. Acclaiming him as Messiah entails believing this, and acclaiming the Law of Scripture entails believing Jesus is the fulfillment of its predictions. But they are one. Even the explosion of the church beyond the cultural and religious boundaries to Gentiles is achieved with minimal modification. Jews and Gentiles of the church fulfill all that the Bible demands of them. And at the heart of that demand is the command to love.

Luke's monument to early ecumenism stands in the New Testament amid companions who saw it very differently. The submerging of the Jewish church would lead to the abandonment of his vision. It is still alive in Justin, who looks to Christ's future reign in Jerusalem (Dial. 80). But the church has lived selectively from the Lukan heritage. It has taken more from Peter's vision; it has disregarded the apostolic decree. It finds more inspiration in Luke's call for justice for the poor than in his ecumenical compromises. Yet Luke's patterns set the structure for the church's year and Luke has retained in a less cluttered way than Matthew our access to anecdotes and sayings that bring us near to the Jesus of history.

JOHN

Sole Loyalty to Life and Truth

The Gospel of John is concerned with the Word from the beginning. "In the beginning was the Word and Word was with God and the Word was God." These words find their echo at the conclusion of the so-called prologue where the author declares: "No one has seen God at any time; the only God who is in the bosom of the Father has made him known" (1:18). The claims are daring and baffling, but they leave us in no doubt: the Word is a person. The Word comes from God, was with God in the beginning. And the relationship with God is such that the Word may also be addressed as God; or, perhaps we should say, addresses us as God.

Word, Wisdom, and the Law

The Word is John's Bible. The Word is Jesus. How then does this Word relate to the written Bible, to the Scriptures and to God's word to Israel in the past? This special piece at the beginning of John's gospel celebrates Jesus in language familiar to Jewish ears of the time. For in writings like Proverbs, Sirach, the Wisdom of Solomon, and in the prolific expositions of Philo of Alexandria, there had developed a strong tradition about God's wisdom and God's word (Prov. 8:22-31; Sirach 24; Wisdom 7:21–8:1; Baruch 3:9–4:1; 1 Enoch 42). God's wisdom — in

123

Greek, *sophia* — became in such traditions more than just an attribute of God. What began perhaps as a daring illustration, wisdom crying aloud on the streets like a woman calling people to enter her house, became something much more. People pictured wisdom as a being beside God, like the highest angel, sometimes much more as God's image or reflection; sometimes almost inseparable from God. The story of Israel's history with God could be told as the story of God's wisdom visiting Israel, through Moses and the prophets and the sages. The story was sometimes very positive: wisdom looked for a place to dwell on earth and found Israel (Sirach 24:8-12; Baruch 3:37). Sometimes it was negative; wisdom looked for a place to dwell and found none (1 Enoch 42).

Wisdom was not only the reflection and image of God's being, God's assistant in creation, the firstborn of God's creation. It also was the one in whom God continued to address Israel. This made it a special way of speaking about the Scriptures, in particular, the Law. God's wisdom is God's word of instruction to Israel. It called people to take upon themselves its yoke (Sirach 51:25-26). When in Matthew Jesus invites people to come to him to bear his yoke he is employing this kind of imagery (Matt. 11:28-30). Indeed, Q contained sayings of Jesus that portrayed John and Jesus and then the prophets and apostles as envoys sent by wisdom (Q 11:49-51; cf. Luke 11:49-51; Matt. 23:34-36; Q 7:35; cf. Luke 7:35; Matt. 11:19). In some forms of the tradition the female image of wisdom, the woman, came to be modified by the use of the word *Logos*, translated as Word (especially in Philo). The Word of God came to Israel.

John's gospel employs this imagery in its famous prologue. Poetic rhythms in parts of the first eighteen verses suggest that the author has made use of such traditions. Perhaps at one stage there had been simply a hymn praising God's wisdom and word as the light and life for human beings which had come to Israel. Certainly before John used it, it had been applied to Jesus. Linking Jesus with the image of the word or wisdom made a lot of sense to many Jewish Christians in the early decades of the church. It was a way of saying: what we identified as God's wisdom we find in Jesus. Thus we find hymns used in Colossians (1:15-20) and Hebrews (1:2-4) which hail Jesus in these terms. He is not only the firstborn from the dead; he is also the firstborn of all creation. He is the image and reflection of God. He is the Son of God with God from the beginning. John will have found such a hymn and reworked it for his grand opening. Jesus is the Word who was with God from the beginning.

It is not only the image of the Word which people applied to God's wisdom. Especially where God's wisdom was identified with God's Law, it became common to speak of Wisdom, God's Law as light and life and truth. It was the water of life, the bread of life (e.g., Sirach 51:25-26). It was the way to life, the gate, the well, the glory and presence of God. These images are all familiar from the Old Testament and from Jewish writings of the period. We know them also because they feature throughout John's gospel. In the gospel Jesus is the light, the life, the truth, the water of life, the bread of life, the way, the gate, the bearer of God's glory. We find these images already in the prologue: in the Word was life and the life was the light for people. The light shines in the darkness and the darkness has not overcome it.

Possibly John found an early Jewish Christian hymn that gave a Christian version of Israel's history. The Word was active in creation, came to Israel, and then finally came in Jesus. The hymn might then have dovetailed Jesus and the Law so completely that Jesus was the embodiment of God's Word, God's Law, and having come to Israel in the past, he now came in a new form in Jesus. God's Law and Jesus' exposition of it are one and the same. It would be a position that would give fine expression to the stance we find in Matthew.

Only Jesus Is the Word, Not the Law

In John however we find something different. John does not use the imagery to speak of successive stages in Israel's history. True, he begins with creation, but then he immediately speaks of the Word as the light and speaks of its shining in the present (1:5). He then makes reference to John the Baptist who bore witness to the light, but was not himself the light, a point on which the author places great emphasis (1:6-8). In other words, throughout the prologue the Word is referring to Jesus as the Word, and except for the opening few verses, it is referring to Jesus' activity in his ministry and in his risen life. This leaves no room to understand Jesus as the Word that came to Israel already through her prophets or through her Law. The Word came to Israel (he came to his own) in Jesus' ministry, and Israel rejected him. Verse 14 then explains that the Word entered our human life so that we could see him and acknowledge who he is, God's only Son, full of grace and truth.

In other words, John has used the imagery to refer to Jesus alone. Jesus alone is the light and life and truth; he is full of grace and truth. Verse 17 explains this further and confirms our finding: "We have all received from this fullness." But then come the words: "grace instead of grace." Their significance is immediately explained: "The Law was given through Moses; grace and truth came through Jesus Christ." Jesus the Word is the bearer of grace and truth. The Word and the Law are not identical. The Word, in fact, replaces the Law. John does not identify the two and have Jesus coming to Israel through the Law and the Prophets during his history. The Word has come only in Jesus. But John also acknowledges the gift of the Law.

Shimmering behind this last section of the Prologue is the account of Moses' ascent up Mount Sinai (Exod. 33:7-23; 34:6). There Moses pitched a tent, and God promised his presence; Moses asked to see God's glory, and God declared his grace. Here in John 1:14 we read: "The Word became flesh and tented among us and we beheld his glory, glory as of the only Son of the Father, full of grace and truth." 1:18 concludes: "No one has seen God at any time; the only God who is in the bosom of the Father has made him known." What Moses longed for has now been made possible. Not only through the fact that someone has seen God, but also through the fact that he makes God's glory visible. In Jesus, John is telling us, we see God. Later he will say: "the one who has seen me has seen the Father."

Jesus tents among us as God's presence. In contrast, Moses did not see God and could not reveal God's glory. Yet Moses still received the Law. What is the point of the contrast? At that time God gave Moses the Law; now through Jesus what Moses could not give has become available. This sheds light on the phrase in 1:16. Instead of one gift we have received another: grace instead of grace. Some have translated the expression as grace upon, that is, in addition to, grace, as if we now have two sources of grace with the new one complementing or supplementing the other. This assumes that the Law and the Word are identical. It is also not the normal meaning of the Greek words. John's position is rather that the Word supplants the Law, as becomes apparent from a close reading of the gospel.

Scripture as Witness to Jesus, the Word

It is interesting to note that none of this entails a disparagement of the Law or its contents. The Law, the heart of the Scriptures, is God's gift. It is gift and grace in that sense. It was given to be valid until Jesus came; but now it is obsolete. In place of true glory Moses received only the Law, a substitute; now the revelation of glory is available, and is available to all. The substitute is no longer needed. Yet John is far from discarding the Scriptures. On the contrary, they play a significant role. Their role is to bear testimony to Jesus. Their function is similar to John the Baptist's. The gospel writer is especially careful to remove all indications that John the Baptist had more significance than this. Listen to 1:20 on the issue of John's identity: John "confessed and did not deny and confessed, 'I am not the Christ.'" There could be no mistake! John points to Jesus. In a similar way the author highlights the primary function of Scripture as testifying to Jesus.

Therefore John is interested in prophetic prediction fulfilled in Jesus. This is usually in general terms: Jesus is the promised Messiah. Philip tells Nathaniel, "We found him of whom Moses in the Law and also the prophets wrote" (1:45). Jesus scolds the Jewish teachers for searching the Scriptures for life but failing to see that they testify to Jesus who is the life (5:39, 46-47; 6:44-46). It is only in this role that the Scriptures are the source of life. By far the most common form is where John indicates that Jesus fulfills messianic hope (e.g., 1:41, 45; 4:25-

26; 12:15). Jesus is the one who was to come. Some of the imagery used of Jesus reflects other imagery of prophetic hope. When John tells how Jesus made water into wine at the wedding feast, many would hear echoes of the prophetic hope for a great banquet at the end of time (e.g., Isa. 25:6). John is saying: in Jesus it has come. When he feeds the five thousand, the miracles of the Exodus are making a return, as many expected they would.

The Jewishness of John's Gospel

John's gospel reflects strong connections with Judaism. John's Jesus now addresses a community that finds itself thrown out of the synagogue and having to make its own way (cf. 16:2; 9:34). Everywhere there are traces of this origin. This is so not only in John's use of Scripture, but also in his familiarity with Jewish traditions of Scripture interpretation. The use of imagery once applied to the Law, but now to Jesus, is further evidence. John also includes considerable incidental detail about Jewish practices, rites, and institutions. He mentions stone jars used for purification (2:6). He alludes to the practice of purification before entering the temple (11:55; 13:10). He mentions most of the festivals. He shows Jesus concerned about what was going on in the temple (2:14-16).

For John, Israel's rites and institutions were not Jewish customs; they were what the Scriptures had commanded. They were not any nation's culture. They were divinely sanctioned. In John's view, the Samaritans had it wrong in locating their temple on Mount Gerizim (4:22). God's salvation had come not through the Samaritans, but through the Jews. In other words, John's comment earlier that the Law was given through Moses is not to be taken lightly. The Law was given by God. The Law is so central that it can at times encompass the whole of Scripture, as it sometimes does in Paul (e.g., John 10:34-35 and 15:25, where Psalm texts are cited as belonging to "the Law." Cf. Rom. 3:10-19). John assumes its authority and depends upon it.

Scriptures: Its Stories Foreshadow Christ

Yet Scripture's role has been radically redefined. We see this at two levels: in the way that John uses its stories and in the way John treats its institutions. We have already noted the allusion to Sinai in the final verses of the prologue. At the end of Chapter 1 we find an allusion to Jacob's dream where he saw a ladder with angels descending and ascending upon it. That imagery now alludes to Christ as the center of the angel's attention. In chapter three we find the analogy between the snake held up by Moses and Jesus' crucifixion and exaltation (3:13-15). Perhaps the most famous analogy is between the manna in the wilderness and Jesus as the bread of life (6:30-58). Jewish tradition had employed the manna as an image of the Law, God's nourishing word for the soul. In John Jesus declares that Moses did not give them manna from heaven; only Jesus gives true manna (6:32). This is typical of John's denial that the Law can be the source of life; only Jesus is that.

The passage is also interesting for the way it employs the Bible story. John is not denying the miracle of the manna; otherwise why mention it? He is using it to say something about Jesus. What is the link between the two events? The answer is: God. God was involved then; God is involved in Jesus. Are there more links? Both are talking about feeding. Is the manna story a prophecy of Jesus' feeding? No; nothing is predicted. Rather John sets one action of God beside the other. Yet there is a sense in which John is using the one story to testify to the other. The manna story serves to testify to Jesus. That is its significance. John is not interested in other details of the story or its history. He is using the story as a parable. It describes an event at one level: the level of ordinary history and a miracle within it. This story becomes a kind of grid or pattern for saying something different, for talking about Jesus. The first story functions as imagery to support what John is saying about Jesus. The interest does not extend beyond that.

Scripture: Its Institutions Foreshadow Christ

We find the same in relation to the institutions based in the Law. The pouring out of water and the lighting of candles form part of the ritual associated with the feast of the tabernacles (7:37-39; 8:12). In the midst of the feast Jesus declares that he offers the water of life and he is the light of the world. What is the connection? It is not that Jesus is try-ing to reform the festival or modify it. Rather it is a source of imagery and that is all. Yet it is a divinely sanctioned source of imagery, because it is founded in Scripture. Yet imagery it is; John is not promoting the festival. Nor does he want to go further and develop a systematic matching between all Jewish festivals and ordinances and Jesus. Just here and there John employs the old as an image foreshadowing the new.

We see the same in the account of Jesus' action in the temple (2:13-22). John indicates that Jesus did in fact have concern for the temple during his ministry, but then indicates that this is going to change. The risen Jesus will replace the temple. The temple is now mere imagery for who Jesus is, nothing more.

We find the same pattern extensively throughout the gospel. John has no interest in defending Jesus' action on the sabbath, because Je-sus is beyond sabbath law (5:16-30). He belongs to God, who in that sense has been resting ever since the seventh day of creation and work-ing only to sustain and restore it. The same is true of Jewish purifica-tion rites. They are left behind because in Jesus there is a new cleansing (2:6; 13:1-17; 15:3). In 3:3, 5 John has Christian baptism in mind, just as elsewhere he envisages symbolic acts that will continue in the church, not least in the eucharist (6:51-58). But Jewish washings, mostly enjoined in Scripture, are a thing of the past. The water of the jars set aside for ritual purification have miraculously become the wine of the new age. Similarly, Jesus is now the only sacrifice that matters, the Passover lamb (1:29).

The Law Superseded

We find nothing in John like Q's statements about the immutability of the Law and its echo in Matthew and Luke. On the one occasion where it looks as if Jesus is offering defense for his actions in terms of the Law, the truth is otherwise. Attacked for having healed the lame man on the sabbath, Jesus points to the practice of circumcising on the sabbath (7:19-24). This is not justification of Jesus' action within the framework of the Law but exposure of the inconsistency of Jesus' opposition. Similarly, where it looks as though Jesus engages in scriptural argument when confronted over his claim to be Son of God, his response is far from that and not a serious argument (10:31-39). The fact that Psalm 82 addresses people as "gods" scarcely justifies Jesus' own use of "Son of God," which in any case means something quite different. Again Jesus is confronting the Jews with their own view of immutable Scripture and exposing their inconsistencies.

Throughout the gospel there is one authority: Jesus. The Scriptures testify to him. That is their sole remaining authority. All other functions have ceased. Israel's stories and institutions, sacred stories and divinely sanctioned institutions, are now a source of symbols, nothing more. The Law is not the light; Jesus is. He is the light and life and truth and bread and water. It is his instruction that informs the disciples, not biblical law. In their new situation Jesus gives the new commandment that they love one another. While we may assume John's community would presuppose the ethical values implied in the Decalogue, they are nowhere cited as guides. At most they are assumed in the charges and countercharges that constitute Jesus' interaction with the Jews. John's Jesus obviously shares such values, but has left the Law behind. It is "their Law," "your Law," a common phrase in John (15:25; 8:17; 10:34). In their foolishness they cling to it when it is no longer appropriate, for what Moses sought has become reality. The glory has been revealed for all to see: in the person of Jesus. Between Jesus and Moses there may be correspondences, but there is no comparison.

Something New of a Higher Order of Reality

The claims made for Jesus underlie John's approach to the Bible. The Son has come from above (3:31-32). He has come from the intimacy of the Father's presence, from the Father's glory (1:18; 17:1-5). This is not an improvement, a new chapter, in ongoing revelation. It is something of a new order altogether. God's gifts to human beings through Moses and the prophets are one thing; the coming of the divine Son is something totally new. It is not just the latest; it is of different quality, divine quality. It belongs to a higher level of reality. This is fundamental to John's thought. The Law addressed people at the level of earthly reality. It gave commands and ordinances, recounted God's actions on earth and ordained earthly institutions. As Jesus explains to the Samaritan woman, the deeper reality of God is of a different order. God is spirit and people worshiping God must do so in spirit and truth (4:23-24). Temples on mountains now cease to have relevance, even though as long as the old order existed, the Samaritans were wrong and the Jews were right (4:22). But now the new has come. There is now true worship. In this incident we come close to Mark's value system, which disparages localizations of the divine; but there is still considerable distance. What Mark declares meaningless, John sees as ordained by God for a time.

This contrast between two levels of reality is fundamental for John's gospel. Faith means moving from one level to the other. Nicodemus remains at the earthly level; to see the kingdom is to see this higher level of reality (3:3). Staying with the stories and institutions of the Law is staying at the lower level like Nicodemus. This framework of thought explains the way John uses the stories and the institutions. Reality at the lower level is not evil; events at that level are not necessarily demonic. In the case of the Scriptures they show the signs of God's action. But all this can now only serve to point beyond that level to Jesus, the true Word. He alone is the way to the Father. These were of the flesh; he is of the Spirit. In John Jesus declares: "The Spirit is life giving; the flesh is no use at all; the words which I speak are spirit and life" (6:63). And earlier: "That which is born of the flesh is flesh, that which is born of the Spirit is Spirit. Do not wonder that I said to you, 'You must be born from above'" (3:6-7).

John's insistence on perceiving this new level of reality also affects the way he uses the events of Jesus' earthly ministry. Miracles are affirmed, but people who follow Jesus or acclaim him only on that basis fail to win his approval. John writes, "Many believed in his name because they saw the miracles he was doing, but Jesus did not trust them" (2:23). This comes immediately before the famous encounter with Nicodemus, who amply illustrates this failure. He tells Jesus, "Rabbi, we know that you are a teacher come from God, because no one can do these miracles which you do unless God is with him" (3:2). Jesus tells him: "Unless a person is born from above, he cannot see the kingdom of God" (3:3). Even Jesus' own ministry is placed within the framework.

John's Radically Different Approach to Scripture

John's gospel offers therefore a radically different approach to Jesus and his attitude towards Scripture. Unlike Mark it does not have Jesus declare parts of Scripture invalid. John treats the institutions and practices of Judaism with respect. Scripture, and, above all, the Law, was God's gift. Its Law came from God. God gave it at the point where Moses sought much more. But now that what Moses sought has become available, the Law ceases its function. Its role now, like the rest of Scripture, with its stories and its institutions, is to point to Christ. This happens directly in prophecies of the Messiah, which Jesus more than fulfills. It happens indirectly as Scripture story and institution provide patterns and images that foreshadow the truth which has come in Jesus. The Scriptures are a rich source of spiritual imagery to portray Christ. For John, only Jesus is the Word. The Law is not the divine Logos. It was God's interim gift until the Word came. The Law and the Scripture are not the life, the light, the truth, the way, the water, the bread, and so on, but at most the witness to the Jesus who is all these things.

Accordingly John's community depends solely on its Christology and only indirectly on the Scriptures as a support for this Christology. Its life is solely centered on the risen Christ made present through the Spirit. Its law is mutual love and love shared with the Son and the Father, not the Old Testament commandments (13:34-35; 15:9-17). Love for the world remains on the books in its most famous phrase, "God so loved the world" (3:16), but mostly the focus is on the community and its members. Mission entails drawing people into this community and its relationships of love. Christ is at its center, not the Law or the Scriptures — except as witness to the Word. These are not the people of the book; they are the people of the Word.

Dangers and Strengths in John's Approach

The massive shift to Christ-centeredness in this way exposes the community to grave dangers. Who defines who this Jesus is and what he wants? The focus on the higher reality exposes the community to the danger that some will despise the lower reality altogether. This, in turn, will lead to playing down the humanity and history of Jesus and disregarding the concrete needs of fellow members of the community. By the time 1 John was written both of these developments have taken place and have split the community (2:18-21, 26-27; 4:1-6). It is interesting that this does not lead to a rehabilitation of Scripture as a source of ethics. Despite the major ethical issues confronting the community the author makes one sole reference to the Old Testament, and that as an analogy: the murderous wrath of Cain (3:12).

Displacing scriptural authority or refashioning it to a subordinate role also creates a vacuum. It is not possible to sustain such an approach without recourse to other tangible sources of authority. The author of the epistle asserts the authority of the tradition bearers, those who were there from the beginning (1:1-4; 2:24-25). The collection of New Testament writings is a larger response to this problem and becomes, in turn, another version of the problem of the authority of Scripture. They become something divine and evoke the same kinds of tensions evident in the story of Jesus and the story of the early church.

The Johannine solution of submerging Scripture under the person of the Word achieves a number of gains. It cut Christianity loose from its cultural moorings in Judaism or, at least, provided the ideological basis for this to happen. This was achieved at awful cost in the case of John's gospel and its interpreters. The intense conflict between Jews — between Jesus and the Johannine Jews and the unbelieving Jews — became already in John a symbol of good against evil, God against the devil (8:37-59). In non-Jewish hands it made the gospel a major tract for an anti-Semitism whose horrendous consequences we can never forget.

On the other hand, it took the Jewish image of God away from its original housing and reset it in a personal context in which the focus became personal relationship. In particular, it wrested Jewish imagery, once attached to its book of command and story, away from the Law and Scripture, and attached it to a person in such a way as to create a new model for spirituality. Light and life and truth and water and bread now no longer symbolize a complex system of ordinances and institutions, but a personal relationship. The Johannine treatment of Jesus also transforms the story of Jesus so that what might have been sets of laws and stories of Jesus, as in Matthew, becomes a single entity. Jesus becomes in John a cipher for God. In exploiting the wisdom myth John creates not a second god, but a figure like ancient wisdom, God's word, who functions effectively as a focal point for devotion to God. Despite his high Christology, or perhaps because of it, John has all but collapsed Jesus' separate identity into God. The result of this process is to put God at the center and to speak of God in terms that have universal appeal: light, life, water, and so on.

This could have led to an abandonment of the Bible altogether and in some circles it would. It did in the gospel of Thomas, as we shall see. For John that is unthinkable, although the author of 1 John gets by with little reference to it. For the writer of the gospel, the Bible with its Law and its stories retains an important place. One aspect of this reflects his theology as we have seen: the Bible preserves prediction as well as defunct law. It also offers a rich source of imagery in its stories and institutions. This divinely sanctioned sourcebook is a treasury for the community. Here we meet an interesting model for appreciating religious tradition. It is perhaps suggestive for today. Distance from biblical law — and in practice we are mostly at one with John in this — need not prevent us from a creative use of the tradition.

Bearers of the biblical tradition, and by that I mean especially its interpreters, can learn from John. Some biblical material is suited well to treatment as story and imagery, without the pressure of having to validate it in some way or demonstrate some continuity with the gospel. In an age in which gospel values will often find themselves in collision with biblical traditions, both old and new, this is one way forward. Can I live with being in a community that feeds from a collections of writings and traditions which I recognize as of very mixed value and with which I react both positively and negatively and still find therein the Word of the Lord? I think I can. It is a rich experience. To bring out the knife on aberrant traditions and imagine one could revise or purify it is to delude oneself. Poetry cannot sustain itself where the measure is bald truth and accuracy. And poetry is life. John's singly focused spirituality lends itself to a creatively positive relationship to the tradition, indeed to our own religion, and frees one to let it be and not pretend as to its authority.

The Gospel of Thomas

Before closing let me mention Thomas. Thomas, a collection of sayings of Jesus from the second century, but often reflecting traditions that must be as early as the canonical gospels, marches beyond the Law. For a document of its kind it is surprisingly occupied with Jewish practices and must reflect a history in which Jewishness was a significant factor. Thus it touches on sabbath, almsgiving, fasting, prayer, food laws, circumcision, purifications, and the temple. It consistently rejects Jewish practices. But many of them it spiritualizes. Fasting becomes a term for strict asceticism over against the world; sabbath, a symbol of permanent rest; circumcision, the life of the Spirit; and the temple, an image of the places of the Father, the heavenly kingdom. To this extent it stands with John, though John is less disparaging. But Thomas goes far beyond John in dismissing all need for scriptural warrant, even the witness of the prophets. Saying 52, for instance, reports the words of the disciples: "Twenty-four prophets spoke in Israel, and they all spoke of you"; to which Jesus responds: "You have abandoned the living one before your eyes, and spoken about the dead."

Attitudes to Scripture in the Gospels

John in some ways offers the most radical approach to Scripture within the gospels, at least in effect, for it greatly reduces its role. Yet John does not go as far as Mark, who has Jesus declare significant aspects of biblical law invalid. John's difference from Q and Matthew is in contrasting Jesus and the Law. His approach has some similarities to Paul; both abandon the Law as demand, yet, on the one hand, John is not prepared to attribute a negative role to the Law (to create servitude; Gal. 3:19) or verge on calling its integrity into question, as does Paul; and on the other hand, Paul continues to cite the ethical commandments quite explicitly and claim a new way of fulfilling them (Gal. 5:13-14). It is interesting that John has not brought issues of the Gentile mission into his equation, though the inclusion of these sheep from another fold is on the horizon of John's account and John knows stories that originally celebrated inclusion in general, at least of women and Samaritans.

John has broken the nexus between old and new which Luke sought to maintain. John reflects an intense history of Jewishness and bitter inner Jewish conflict and then inner community conflict; Luke tells of conflicts at a distance and admires a divinely sanctioned culture that has continuing validity and with whose hopes he identifies. All emphasize the priority of love in the working out of what God demands; but in John the preoccupation is love within the group. Love is the only demand; so there is no issue of using it as a criterion to interpret scriptural law. Loyalty to Jesus and to God is in danger of replacing compassion for all with a new formal structure of authority.

CONCLUSION

Interpreting Scripture Today

Jesus and the Gospels

The differing responses of the gospel writers reveal differing situations. They give the lie to the notion that the gospel writers had a single attitude towards Scripture and its Law. Even Q and Matthew and Luke, who in various ways stress the immutability of Scripture and its authority, are far from espousing literalism or an approach that would portray God as more interested in laws than in people. Rather, people matter most.

This approach, evident in all the gospels, perhaps only faintly in John, appears to derive from Jesus' own practice. It stands in conflict with approaches which reason that the focus should be meeting God's demands as a set of instructions and rules. The sabbath, like the rest of the Law's provisions, was made for people, not people for the sabbath. Jesus' approach was less scribal than Matthew's. It appealed to scriptural and day-to-day imagery after the model of wisdom teachers to point to the attitudes and behaviors that characterize the kingdom, rather than to biblical texts. Jesus was more like a teacher of wisdom than a scribe.

The stances of the gospel writers, various as they are, were worked out over against positions recognizable then and in our own day, which insist that if God said it we must obey and no one is to question

138

that God said it. Thus Mark drew the implication from Jesus' approach that it authorized the dismantling of all barriers of discrimination — including those enshrined in Scripture — against fellow human beings, at least in relation to non-Jews.

Luke, for his part, knew this had happened with regard to circumcision, but sought to rehabilitate Christianity and to show it as deviant from biblical authority only in this single divinely sanctioned respect. He champions the view that the biblical law frees Gentiles also from much else so that they can maintain faithfulness to the Law while being to a large degree, in reality, nonobservant. This is perhaps Luke's fiction, but I think he believed it.

Following the lead of Q, Matthew also defends Jesus against the charge that he set aside any part of the Law, but Matthew's concerns are strongly Jewish and deal with accusations leveled at his Jewish Christian community in a predominantly Jewish society. Nevertheless, Matthew's Jesus has a clear hierarchy of values, whose strength would inevitably lead to a position closer to Luke and even Mark, especially as Gentile numbers increased; but it had not yet reached this point.

John has no such qualms. Integrity is solved in the context of a new stage in God's action in history, which finally reveals what the former stage could only foreshadow in image. It is a stance not dissimilar to that of the epistle to the Hebrews, but there the focus is largely the sacrificial cult; it is worked out in terminology that merged popular Platonism and apocalyptic thought. For John, Christ rules and rules alone; Law and Scripture survive only as witnesses and relics of a defunct order which now, through its ordinances and stories, provides imagery that must have worked well for former Jews, but for others would have largely retired into oblivion except for its universal themes. The Johannine solution leaves a vacuum, and the community's history testifies to what filled it. One aspect of that history is its integration within a collection of gospels in which feet are kept on the ground and Jesus is still real.

John closes the circle, or, perhaps better, hangs on the cluster which despite its odd shapes and sizes has become a source of nourishment and controversy in the church. It is not for us to emulate their solutions or crucify those who want to wrestle with their use compassionately. But they, at least, expose the need for such wrestling and why it is so fiercely resisted. They also have a way of mediating what must have been Jesus' own vision and so provide bread and wine for our journey today.

Unity and Room for Diversity

The diversity within the cluster is part of the richness of Scripture. We may be glad that Christians of the early centuries did not seek to impose exact conformity on the collection of accounts of Jesus' life. Only one gospel might have survived, not four. The unity that exists among them is a unity that tolerates diversity only because what they have in common outweighs what distinguishes them. It is a unity that might symbolize unity in and among the churches. For faith is never best defined in exact terms, just as God can never be captured in an image of the hands or the mind. It is an acknowledgment of the truth that we must always live with an awareness of our limits.

The issue this study raises goes beyond affirming diversity in unity. For all of the gospels have in common an attitude towards Scripture and tradition. This attitude stands in contrast to what we popularly understand by "fundamentalism." In fact, it reflects that the gospel writers saw Jesus, and doubtless understood themselves, to be in conflict with that kind of fundamentalism. Indeed they would have us believe that it was this kind of fundamentalism which led to Jesus' crucifixion. Historical reality is more complex than such a simple equation allows.

Working with Priorities

Nevertheless there can be little doubt that the conflict over interpretation of Scripture, both in the ministry of Jesus and in the life of the church, did have to do with whether people were prepared to differentiate within Scripture and where people set priorities. Approaches that set all at the same level as equally to be observed because given by God faced rejection. For some, as originally for Jesus, setting priorities was a matter of upholding Scripture and its commands in their entirety, but of affirming love for God and one's neighbor as the greatest commandments. Even then this approach refused to allow love for God to sanction an attitude of fundamentalism which would argue that if God said it, then every command must be obeyed without question. In other words, it worked with a theology that saw the central issue of relating to God not as obeying commands but as sharing God's attitudes, which come to expression in commands but in more than that.

Even many people who call themselves "fundamentalist" and explain their position in conformity with the popular understanding of the term do not uphold this stance consistently. There are value systems that operate as hidden axioms in their interpretation. They will place greater emphasis on some areas rather than others. For instance, they may interpret sabbath law (usually transferred to Sunday) rather lightly, while insisting on punctilious observance of moral laws or of instructions concerning women or dress. There are few real fundamentalists who apply the line consistently, yet there are many who appeal to it as an ideology and as being basic to Christianity, Bible believing.

Beyond Priorities

The inclusive stance that upheld the whole of Scripture, but weighed some parts above others, could scarcely survive as the church faced new realities and felt driven by the weightier elements. In Matthew you sense the strain as he tries to hold it all together, although even then it is clear where Matthew puts the emphasis. Much of the Law has disappeared from view. Luke also tries to hold it all together, but does so without the sense of strain, because Luke's context appears to be that of a largely Gentile church which can afford to paint a picture of unity on a grand scale. Matthew, by contrast, reflects a community of largely Jewish believers facing marginalization within a Jewish context and struggling to retain new positions while defending itself against charges of apostasy from Israel.

In other words, for Luke the problem has resolved itself and he can afford to paint a generous and tolerant picture. For Matthew the problem is still acute. But both hold firmly to the priorities set by Jesus: compassion for people is the underlying principle when interpreting Scripture, not obedience to commands. In Mark we saw how these priorities have challenged parts of Scripture itself. Demands of the Law that provided obstacles in the path of including Gentiles have fallen, as they had with Paul. The cultic and ceremonial has been declared irrelevant. Inclusion of all people has meant exclusion of whatever stands in its way, including commands the Bible declares to be God's demand.

John has gone far further. Not only are some parts of the Law set aside. The Law itself is set aside and its authority replaced by Jesus. Yet in doing so John, unlike Mark, does not deem the commands irrelevant because such outward concerns with food and circumcision and the like were never valid, but because they have now been superseded. In this respect John is in some ways closer to Paul than is Mark. Both John and Paul work within a pattern according to which one God-given order is replaced by another. Mark is more radical, declaring that aspects of the one order never were relevant. Paul comes close to this when he declares that only circumcision of the heart is relevant (Rom. 2:25-29), but otherwise he runs with the view that the Law was God's gift and ceases to apply.

Both "Conservative" and "Liberal"

The gospels exhibit, therefore, considerable diversity in their approaches to Scripture. Religion generally tends to be conservative, in the sense that it preserves established values. We see this conservative tendency coming to expression in different ways in both Matthew and Luke. It is also a fundamentally conservative strategy to explain change in terms of divinely ordained epochs in history, such as we find in Paul and John. This is part of valuing the old and of acknowledging God's action in the past and at the same time of claiming that it is this God who is acting in the present and in the new.

"Conservative" in this sense is not a negative slogan, but a characteristic of Christian faith. Yet, to use another slogan word, "liberal," the tendency throughout all the gospels is towards a liberal interpretation of Scripture. That is, the tendency is to show freedom in applying Scripture and its insights to new situations. This freedom comes, at the same time, from a kind of conservatism. It seeks to conserve underlying values and differs from the conservatism that seeks to conserve the letter of the Law. The dispute between these two approaches comes to expression in Paul's own slogans: letter or spirit.

The liberal approach to Scripture in this sense has shown itself in the willingness of people not only to avow love for God and love for people as fundamental values, but also to continue to abandon some scriptural commands and views because of it. It was this approach that led to abolition of slavery, gave women a voice in church and community, and finally led to the ordination of women in many traditions. Sometimes such liberal positions have been espoused because people have convinced themselves that former interpretation of the relevant Scripture passages was wrong and that in opting for the new positions they are still following the letter of Scripture, but this is largely self-deception. It is more honest to stand with Mark and acknowledge that to take an inclusive stance means to depart from some biblical injunctions.

Confronting Fundamental Values

The issue is much larger than the matter of slavery, the role of women in family and community, sexual roles and practices, and the like, although in each of these and in many others besides we need, I believe, the kind of critical appreciation that underlies Mark's approach. The issue of interpreting Scripture today is about more than whether you agree with a biblical writer's stance on homosexuality or a writer's alleged inspiration in claiming that God has declared this or that behavior acceptable. It is not just a matter of a command or a view here or there within Scripture, but of the ethos of Scripture itself. To begin with, it is largely male in its interests and doubtless its authorship. But the issue is much greater than that.

The writers of the Bible belonged to cultures and subcultures that embodied certain values reflecting the social system of the day. In these women were largely inferior, but so also were a good many others. And generally power and wealth was in the hands of a very few, with the rest surviving because they were locked into dependence on favors from their superiors. It was a world in which life was cheap. The great person was the ruler, the wealthy person. Even the language of the poor and pious enshrines and so reinforces these values. It was a largely closed system from which there was no escape. There was no such thing as democracy and no, or very little, respect for human rights.

The system affected the way people thought about the gods, and this in turn reinforced the system. Even in Israel this is the case. The favored terms for God were drawn from the language of the royal courts and houses of power. Gods could destroy at will. Israel's God would authorize destruction of masses of human beings and threaten the same against all dissent. Underlying this is the view that human life is dispensable. The same values continue to determine the views of Christian writers about judgment and damnation. People are ultimately dispensable.

A Wriggling in the System

Yet all the while there is a wriggling in the system. That wriggling is part of the creative challenge to the system whose voice is heard in the prophets and elsewhere where there is protest against the low view of human life the system perpetuates. I prefer to speak of a wriggling in the system because of the complexity of what was going on. The story that God had compassion on Israel and heard its needy cries is a major reverse in the system. Much of Scripture is celebrating such moments of subversion. God rescues slaves out of Egypt. God chooses the lowly shepherd boy, David. Jesus is born in a shelter for animals. At times we seem to see the wriggling new life breaking the shell of the egg, ready to burst forth into free life. Yet these moments remain within a web of oppression. There is joy over the slaughter of Egypt's children and its pursuing army. David will destroy his foes. To reject Jesus warrants everlasting torment.

To read the Bible like this is to be aware of the struggle. It is the struggle of compassion against hate, of life against death. It so penetrates the biblical writings because they belong to a world where the same kind of struggle was going on and largely being lost. When you approach them with this awareness, you can see that in themselves the Scriptures are capable of giving a wide range of messages and of supporting — indeed, promoting — both sides of the struggle. This is why people have found in the Bible inspiration for violence and war. It is why Christians have sometimes been comfortable about slaughter. After all, if God will in the end contrive mass slaughter of the wicked, surely that justifies our destruction of the wicked. It is only a matter of timing. The situation becomes very confused when, effectively, the threat is made that unless you learn to love like Jesus, God will destroy you. It also explains why Christian families can sometimes be places of violence and abuse. Their heavenly Father is not really a good example.

Yet Jesus' stories about decent and caring fathers are part of the subversion he brings. He also set a small child before the disciples and spoke of greatness as lowliness and compassion. He even set it in direct contrast to the values of his day, identifying kings and rulers. Jesus gave expression to the compassion side of the struggle. It was not totally new. Later, Matthew rightly identified it with Hosea's claim that God wanted mercy, not sacrifice. We see how it is primarily this respect and care for people that determined the way Jesus interpreted his own religious tradition. People matter most.

Interpreting Scripture Today

The interpreter today, whether preacher or educator, needs to be aware that the Christian Bible encompasses a range of values, some of which are destructive, some of which bring life. I can remember as a young man being offended by the Porgy and Bess lyric, "It ain't necessarily so. It ain't necessarily so. The things that you're liable to read in the Bible they ain't necessarily so." But it is true, both historically and in terms of values. Yet this can be true without the Bible losing its worth as the source of creative life and positive meaning. It cannot be unmixed. It cannot be sanitized of its violence and prejudice. But handled with sensitivity to the struggle it embodies, it can be a voice for compassion; it can wriggle and struggle its way into our own reality. It can be God's word to us.

The great strength of the gospel writers is their sensitivity to what were Jesus' concerns, especially to what were Jesus' priorities. In that sense they offer us models of how to interpret our religious tradition, including their accounts of Jesus. They all let us know, however conservatively or radically, that for Jesus people mattered most, that compassion was uppermost, and that this was the nature of God's being.

When we approach Scripture like this, the wriggles of the system are seen for the struggles that they are, struggles of compassion waiting to be born. The miracle of inspiration is that for many these are moments when compassion is born. This is what keeps us going. This is what makes Scripture holy. The task of the interpreter is to lead people to these moments. But that means acknowledging the struggle and facing up to the system. In this we are part of a new struggle, for the old system is still largely intact in the modern world, and much of the time our best moments are mere wriggles against its power.

Not to acknowledge that we too are part of the system — and not to acknowledge the struggle present in Scripture — is to expose people to the range of values on both sides of the struggle for their good and harm. To develop a critical appreciation of Scripture and to promote such a stance in others is to participate in the struggle in our own time. It is to follow Jesus and the gospel writers in giving voice to compassion and rejoicing at its birth.

For Further Reading

The following is a selection of major works related to the theme of Jesus and the Law, including those in foreign languages.

Banks, R., *Jesus and the Law in the Synoptic Tradition*, SNTSMS 28 (Cambridge: Cambridge University Press, 1975).

Barth, G., "Matthew's Understanding of the Law" in G. Bornkamm, G. Barth, and H. J. Held, *Tradition and Interpretation in Matthew*, 2nd ed. (London: SCM, 1963, 1982), pp. 58-164.

Berger, K., *Die Gesetzesauslegung Jesu: Ihr historischer Hintergrund im Judentum und im Alten Testament. Teil I: Markus und Parallelen*, WMANT 40. Neukirchen-Vluyn: Neukirchener, 1972 — on Mark and parallels. Only volume 1 has appeared.

Betz, H. D., *The Sermon on the Mount*, Hermeneia (Minneapolis: Fortress, 1995).

Blomberg, C. L., "The Law in Luke-Acts," *Journal for the Study of the New Testament* 22 (1984): 53-80.

Booth, R. P., *Jesus and the Laws of Purity: Tradition History and Legal History in Mark 7*, JSNTS 13 (Sheffield: JSOT Press, 1986).

Broer, I., ed., *Jesus und das jüdische Gesetz* (Stuttgart: Kohlhammer, 1992). In this volume: Broer, I., "Jesus und das Gesetz. Anmerkungen zur Geschichte des Problems und zur Frage der Sündenvergebung durch den historischen Jesus," pp. 61-104; Dautzenberg, G., "Über die Eigenart des Konfliktes, der von jüdischer Seite im Prozess Jesu ausgetragen wurde," pp. 147-72; Müller, K., "Beobachtungen zum Verhältnis von Tora und Halacha in frühjüdischen Quellen," pp. 105-34.

147

Catchpole, D. R., *The Quest for Q* (Edinburgh: T. & T. Clark, 1993).

Crossan, J. D., *The Historical Jesus: The Life of a Mediterranean Jewish Peasant* (San Francisco: Harper, 1991).

Deutsch, C., *Hidden Wisdom and the Easy Yoke: Wisdom, Torah and Discipleship in Matthew 11:25-30*, JSNTSS 18 (Sheffield: JSOT Press, 1987).

Dunn, J. D. G., *Jesus, Paul and the Law: Studies in Mark and Galatians* (London: SPCK, 1990), especially "Jesus and Ritual Purity: A Study of the Tradition-History of Mark 7:15," pp. 37-60; "Mark 2:1–3:6: A Bridge Between Jesus and Paul on the Question of the Law," pp. 10-36.

Dunn, J. D. G., *The Partings of the Ways: Between Christianity and Judaism and Their Significance for the Character of Christianity* (London: SCM, 1991).

Esler, P., *Community and Gospel in Luke-Acts: The Social and Political Motivations of Lucan Theology*, SNTSMS 57 (Cambridge: Cambridge University Press, 1987).

Evans, C. A., "Jesus' Action in the Temple: Cleansing or Portent of Destruction?" *Catholic Biblical Quarterly* 51 (1989): 237-70.

Fitzmyer, J. A., "The Jewish People and the Mosaic Law in Luke-Acts" in Fitzmyer, J. A., *Luke the Theologian: Aspects of His Teaching* (London: Chapman, 1989).

Freyne, S., *Galilee, Jesus, and the Gospels: Literary Approaches and Historical Investigations* (Philadelphia: Fortress, 1988).

Hengel, M. and Deines, R., "E. P. Sanders' 'Common Judaism,' Jesus, and the Pharisees," *Journal of Theological Studies* 46 (1995): 1-70.

Hengel, M., *The 'Hellenization' of Judaea in the First Century after Christ* (London: SCM; Philadelphia: Trinity, 1990).

Hübner, H., *Das Gesetz in der synoptischen Tradition* (Witten: Luther-Verlag, 1973; 2nd ed., Göttingen: Vandenhoeck und Ruprecht, 1986).

Hummel, R., *Die Auseinandersetzung zwischen Kirche und Judentum im Matthäusevangelium*, BETh. 33 (Munich: Kaiser, 1966).

Jervell, J., "The Law in Luke-Acts" in *Luke and the People of God: A New Look at Luke-Acts* (Minneapolis: Augsburg, 1972), pp. 133-52.

Kertelge, K., ed., *Das Gesetz im Neuen Testament*, QD 108 (Freiburg: Herder, 1986). In this volume: Broer, I., "Anmerkungen zum Gesetzesverständnis des Matthäus," pp. 128-45; Dautzenberg, G. "Gesetzeskritik und Gesetzesgehorsam in der Jesustradition," pp. 46-70; Müller, K. "Gesetz und Gesetzeserfüllung im Frühjudentum," pp. 11-27.

Klinghardt, M., *Gesetz und Volk Gottes: Das lukanische Verständnis des Gesetzes*, WUNT 32 (Tübingen: Mohr, 1988).

Kloppenborg, J. S., "Nomos and Ethos in Q" in J. E. Goehring et al., eds., *Chris-*

tian Origins and Christian Beginnings in Honor of James M. Robinson (Sonoma, Calif.: Polebridge, 1990), pp. 35-48.

Kosch, D., *Die eschatologische Tora des Menschensohnes: Untersuchungen zur Rezeption der Stellung Jesu zur Tora in Q*, NovTest et OrbAnt 12 (Göttingen: Vandenhoeck und Ruprecht, 1989).

Kotila, M., *Umstrittene Zeuge: Studien zur Stellung des Gesetzes in der johanneischen Theologiegeschichte*, Annales Academiae Scientiarum Fennicae: Dissertationes Humanarum Litterarum 48 (Helsinki: Suomalainen Tiedeakatemia, 1988).

Lindars, B., ed., *Law and Religion: Essays on the Place of the Law in Israel and Early Christianity* (Cambridge: Clarke, 1988). In this volume: Alexander, P. S., "Jewish Law in the Time of Jesus: Towards a Clarification of the Problem," pp. 44-58; Bauckham, R. J., "Jesus' demonstration in the temple," pp. 72-89; Lindars, B. "All Foods Clean: Thoughts on Jesus and the Law," pp. 61-71; Tuckett, C. M., "Q, the Law and Judaism," pp. 90-101.

Loader, W. R. G., "Challenged at the Boundaries: A Conservative Jesus in Mark's Tradition," *Journal for the Study of the New Testament* 63 (1996): 45-61.

Loader, W. R. G., "Hellenism and the Abandonment of Particularism in Jesus and Paul," *Pacifica* 4 (1991): 245-56.

Loader, W. R. G., *Jesus' Attitude Towards the Law: A Study of the Gospels* (Grand Rapids: Eerdmans, forthcoming; originally in the series: Wissenschaftliche Untersuchungen zum Neuen Testament 2.97, Tübingen: Mohr Siebeck, 1997).

Luz, U., in R. Smend and U. Luz, *Gesetz* Kohlhammer Taschenbücher — Biblische Konfrontationen 1015 (Stuttgart: Kohlhammer, 1981), pp. 58-156.

Menninger, R. E., *Israel and the Church in the Gospel of Matthew*, American University, St. VII, 162 (New York: Peter Lang, 1994).

Mohrlang, R., *Matthew and Paul: A Comparison of Ethical Perspectives*, SNTSMS 48 (Cambridge: Cambridge University Press, 1984).

Müller, K., "Möglichkeit und Vollzug jüdischer Kapitalgerichtsbarkeit im Prozess gegen Jesus von Nazaret" in K. Kertelge, ed., *Der Prozess gegen Jesus: Historische Rückfrage und theologische Deutung*, QD 112 (Freiburg: Herder, 1988), pp. 84-110.

Neusner, J., *Judaism in the Beginning of Christianity* (London: SPCK, 1984).

Neyrey, J. H., "The Idea of Purity in Mark's Gospel," *Semeia* 35 (1986): 91-128.

Overman, J. A., *Matthew's Gospel and Formative Judaism: The Social World of the Matthean Community* (Minneapolis: Fortress, 1990).

Pancaro, S., *The Law in the Fourth Gospel: The Torah and the Gospel, Moses and Jesus,*

Judaism and Christianity According to John, SuppNovT 42 (Leiden: Brill, 1975).

Robinson, J. M., "The International Q Project," *Journal of Biblical Literature* 109 (1990): 499-501; 110 (1991): 494-98; 111 (1992): 500-508; 112 (1993): 500-506; 113 (1994): 495-500; 114 (1995), pp. 475-85. I have largely employed the following *symbols* which the group used: 1. '. . .' indicates probability that text existed here in Q, but is no longer recoverable with sufficient probability; 2. '[[ ]]' The reconstructed text has a probability of C on a scale from A to D. Readings with a probability of D are not included at all; 3. '< >' indicates conjectural emendation found neither in Matthew nor Luke; 4. '<< >>' indicates a train of thought, though the exact Greek text is irrecoverable.

Saldarini, A. J., *Matthew's Christian-Jewish Community* (Chicago: University of Chicago Press, 1994).

Salo, K., *Luke's Treatment of the Law: A Redaction-Critical Investigation,* Annales Academiae Scientiarum Fennicae Dissertationes Humanarum Litterarum 57 (Helsinki: Suomalainen Tiedeakatemia, 1991).

Sanders, E. P., *Jesus and Judaism* (London: SCM, 1985).

Sanders, E. P., *Jewish Law from Jesus to the Mishnah* (London: SCM; Philadelphia: Trinity, 1990).

Sanders, E. P., *The Historical Figure of Jesus* (London: Pengion, 1993).

Sariola, H., *Markus und das Gesetz: Eine redaktionsgeschichtliche Untersuchung,* Annales Academiae Scientiarum Fennicae Dissertationes Humanarum Litterarum 56 (Helsinki: Suomalainen Tiedeakatemia, 1990).

Segal, A. F., "Matthew's Jewish Voice" in D. L. Balch, ed., *The Social History of the Matthean Community: Cross-Disciplinary Approaches* (Minneapolis: Fortress, 1991), pp. 3-37.

Sigal, P., *The Halakah of Jesus of Nazareth According to the Gospel of Matthew* (Lanham, Md.: University of America Press, 1986).

Stanton, G. N., *A Gospel for a New People: Studies in Matthew* (Edinburgh: T. & T. Clark, 1992).

Turner, M. M. B., "The Sabbath, Sunday, and the Law in Luke/Acts" in D. Carson, ed., *From Sabbath to Lord's Day: A Biblical, Historical and Theological Investigation* (Grand Rapids: Zondervan, 1982), pp. 99-157.

Uro, R., *Sheep Among the Wolves: A Study on the Mission Instructions of Q,* Annales Academiae Scientiarum Fennicae Dissertationes Humanarum Litterarum 47 (Helsinki: Suomalainen Tiedeakatemia, 1987).

Vermes, G., *The Religion of Jesus the Jew* (Minneapolis: Fortress, 1993).

Vouga, F., *Jésus et la Loi selon la Tradition synoptique,* Le Monde de la Bible (Genève: Labor et Fides, 1988).

Westerholm, S., *Jesus and Scribal Authority,* Coniectanea Biblica NT Ser 10 (Lund: Gleerup, 1978).

Wilson, S. G., *Luke and the Law,* SNTSMS 50 (Cambridge: Cambridge University Press, 1983).

Yee, G. A., *Jewish Feasts and the Gospel of John,* Zacchaeus Studies: New Testament (Wilmington, Del.: Glazier, 1989).

Scripture Reference Index